Investing in a Rising Interest Rate Environment: Strategies and tips

CLARA CAPITAL

Contents

VIII   Future of Investing in a Rising Interest Rate Environment

I

Understanding Interest Rates

1

Overview

In order to understand the concept of interest rates in the context of investing in a rising interest rate environment, it is essential to have a solid understanding of what interest rates are and how they impact investments.

Interest rates can be thought of as the cost of borrowing money or the return on lending money. They are determined by various factors, including market conditions, central bank policies, inflation, and the overall state of the economy. When interest rates rise, it means that the cost of borrowing increases, making it more expensive for individuals and businesses to obtain loans.

Investing in a rising interest rate environment requires careful consideration and a strategic approach. Here are some key points to keep in mind:

1. Impact on bond prices:

Interest rates and bond prices have an inverse relationship. When interest rates rise, the prices of existing bonds typically decline. This happens because new bonds issued in the higher interest rate environment offer higher yields, making existing bonds with lower interest rates less attractive to investors. Therefore, bond investments may experience capital losses during periods of rising interest rates.

2. Sector-specific considerations:

Different sectors of the economy respond differently to rising interest rates. For example, sectors such as utilities and real estate investment trusts (REITs), which are known for their dividend yields, may be negatively affected as higher interest rates make their yields less attractive compared to fixed-income investments. On the other hand, financial institutions and insurance companies may benefit from higher interest rates as they generate more profit from the spread between borrowing and lending rates.

3. Diversification:

Diversifying investments across different asset classes can help mitigate the impact of rising interest rates. By spreading investments across stocks, bonds, commodities, and real estate, investors can potentially reduce the exposure to any one particular asset class that may be directly affected by interest rate fluctuations.

4. Economic outlook and inflation:

Understanding the economic outlook and inflation trends is crucial when investing in a rising interest rate environment. Rising interest rates are often associated with inflation concerns. Investors may need to consider adjusting their investment strategies to include assets that may provide a hedge against inflation, such as inflation-protected bonds or commodities like gold.

5. Opportunity in fixed-income investments:

While rising interest rates may pose challenges for existing bonds, they can also create opportunities for investors. As interest rates increase, new bonds are issued with higher yields, providing the potential for increased income for fixed-income investors. This could be advantageous for those seeking higher returns in a rising interest rate environment.

Ultimately, investing in a rising interest rate environment requires careful analysis, understanding of economic trends, and an awareness of the potential impacts on different investment sectors. It is important for investors to assess their risk tolerance, consider diversification strategies, and stay informed about market conditions to make informed investment decisions in such an environment. Consulting with a financial advisor or conducting thorough research can further enhance the understanding and decision-making process.

2

Definition of Interest Rates

Interest rates play a crucial role in the world of finance and investing. They are a critical factor to consider when making investment decisions, especially in a rising interest rate environment. This overview aims to provide a simple yet extensive understanding of interest rates and their implications for investors.

Definition of Interest Rates:

In its simplest form, an interest rate is the cost of borrowing or the return on investment for lenders. It represents the percentage of the loan amount that must be paid back on top of the principal. In the context of investing, interest rates can refer to various types, such as mortgage rates, bond yields, or the rate of return on savings accounts.

Rising Interest Rate Environment:

A rising interest rate environment occurs when the prevailing interest rates in the economy are increasing over time. This can happen due to numerous factors, including central bank policies, inflation expectations, and economic growth. When interest rates rise, it affects various aspects of the economy, including consumer spending, borrowing costs, and investment strategies.

Implications for Investors:

Investors need to be aware of the implications of a rising interest rate environment, as it can significantly influence investment decisions. Here are some key points to consider:

1. Bond Investments:

When interest rates rise, the prices of existing bonds tend to fall. This is because new bonds issued in the rising rate environment offer higher yields, making existing bonds less attractive. It is crucial for bond investors to understand the inverse relationship between bond prices and interest rates. However, bonds with longer maturities generally experience more significant price declines than those with shorter maturities.

2. Equity Investments:

In a rising interest rate environment, equity investments can be influenced by multiple factors. Firstly, higher interest rates may increase borrowing costs for companies, potentially impacting their profitability. Additionally, higher-yield bonds may compete more favorably with stocks, attracting investors away from equities. However, rising interest rates often coincide with a healthy economy, which can positively impact corporate earnings and support stock market growth.

3. Real Estate Investments:

Real estate investments are sensitive to interest rates, particularly mortgage rates. Rising interest rates tend to increase borrowing costs for homebuyers, thereby reducing demand for real estate. This can lead to a slowdown in price appreciation or even modest declines in property values. Furthermore, as mortgage rates rise, the affordability of new purchases may decrease, impacting the rental market.

4. Savings and Cash Investments:

A rising interest rate environment is generally favorable for savers and cash investments. Higher interest rates result in increased returns on savings accounts, certificates of deposit (CDs), or money market accounts. This can be particularly beneficial for risk-averse investors seeking income generation or capital preservation. However, the relative attractiveness of cash investments compared to other asset classes may change depending on the rate of return and investment goals.

Conclusion:

Understanding interest rates is essential when navigating the intricacies of investing in a rising interest rate environment. Investors should consider the specific implications for various asset classes, evaluate the risk-return trade-off, and adjust their investment strategies accordingly. Adapting to changing interest rate dynamics is crucial for optimizing investment outcomes and maximizing financial well-being.

3

Types of Interest Rates

To navigate the intricacies of interest rates, it is important to distinguish between nominal and real interest rates.

1. Nominal Interest Rates:

Nominal interest rates refer to the stated or advertised rates charged on loans or offered on investments without accounting for the impact of inflation. For instance, if you have a savings account with a nominal interest rate of 4%, it means your money will grow by 4% annually before considering inflation. Nominal rates are typically what you see when banking institutions promote their products.

2. Real Interest Rates:

Real interest rates take inflation into account, providing a more accurate measure of the true cost of borrowing or return on investment. They represent the difference between the nominal interest rate and the inflation rate. For example, if the nominal interest rate is 4% and the inflation rate is 2%, the real interest rate would be 2%. Real interest rates are crucial for assessing the purchasing power of money over time and the true return on investment.

In a rising interest rate environment, investors should consider how various types of investments may be affected:

1. Bonds:

Bonds are fixed-income securities issued by governments, municipalities, or corporations to raise capital. When interest rates rise, newly issued bonds offer higher yields to attract investors. However, existing bonds with lower yields become less attractive by comparison, potentially leading to a decline in their market value. This phenomenon is known as interest rate risk, which bond investors need to consider when investing in a rising interest rate environment.

2. Stocks:

When interest rates increase, borrowing becomes more expensive, which can impact businesses' profitability, especially those reliant on debt financing. Additionally, higher interest rates might lead investors to shift their focus towards fixed-income investments with relatively less risk. Consequently, stock prices may become more volatile as investors reassess their investment strategies.

3. Real Estate:

Higher interest rates often translate to increased mortgage rates, making homeownership more expensive. This can affect the demand for real estate, potentially leading to a slowdown in the housing market. Additionally, commercial real estate investors may experience higher borrowing costs, potentially impacting property valuations and rental income.

4. Savings and Loan Rates:

In a rising interest rate environment, savings accounts and other fixed-income investments may offer higher yields. However, borrowers will face increased borrowing costs, affecting loans, credit card rates, and other forms of credit. Consequently, consumers may experience tighter financial conditions.

As an investor, it is crucial to consider the type of investment, risk tolerance, and investment horizon before making decisions in a rising interest rate environment. It is advisable to consult with financial professionals to assess and adapt your investment strategy accordingly.

Understanding the intricacies of interest rates and their impact on different investment avenues empowers investors to make informed decisions. By comprehending the nuances of nominal and real interest rates and their implications for various asset classes, investors can navigate the challenges and opportunities presented by a rising interest rate environment.

4

Factors Affecting Interest Rates

In a rising interest rate environment, the rates for borrowing money increase across various financial instruments, including mortgages, loans, and bonds. This rise can be driven by a range of factors, the most prominent being the actions of central banks, market expectations, and the overall state of the economy.

One of the primary drivers of interest rates is monetary policy implemented by central banks. Central banks, such as the Federal Reserve in the United States, set benchmark interest rates to influence borrowing costs, stimulate or cool down economic activity, and manage inflation. When the economy is expanding rapidly, central banks may decide to increase interest rates to curb excessive borrowing and potential inflationary pressures. Therefore, in a rising interest rate environment, central bank decisions are a major factor.

Market expectations also significantly impact interest rates. Expectations about future economic performance and inflation can drive investors' decisions, leading to changes in interest rates. If investors anticipate higher inflation, they may demand higher interest rates to compensate for the anticipated loss in purchasing power of their investments. Furthermore, changes in market expectations regarding economic growth, political stability, or global events can influence interest rates.

The overall state of the economy also affects interest rates in a rising interest rate environment. Factors like employment rates, GDP growth, productivity levels, and inflationary pressures play a critical role in determining interest rate movements. If the economy strengthens, interest rates tend to rise as borrowing costs increase, reflecting increased demand for capital and potential inflationary risks. In contrast, in a weak or recessionary environment, central banks may lower interest rates to stimulate economic growth.

Now, let's explore the implications for investors in a rising interest rate environment. Rising interest rates have repercussions across various investment categories:

1. Bonds:

As interest rates rise, the prices of existing bonds tend to decrease. This inverse relationship is due to new fixed-income securities offering higher yields, reducing the attractiveness of existing bonds with lower coupon rates. Therefore, investors holding fixed-rate bonds may experience capital losses if they sell before maturity. However, rising interest rates can benefit investors with a long-term investment horizon, as they can reinvest their coupon payments at higher rates.

2. Stocks:

Rising interest rates can have mixed effects on the stock market. On one hand, it can increase borrowing costs for companies, potentially leading to reduced profitability and lower stock prices. On the other hand, a strong economy associated with rising interest rates can boost corporate earnings and, consequently, support higher stock valuations. The impact of rising interest rates on stocks may vary depending on the industry, company specifics, and market conditions.

3. Real Estate:

The real estate market is highly sensitive to interest rate movements. Rising interest rates can increase borrowing costs for homebuyers and potentially lower the demand for real estate, leading to decreased property values. However, it is important to note that the impact on real estate can vary based on location, local market conditions, and the overall supply-demand dynamics.

4. Commodities:

Commodity prices can be influenced by interest rate changes, with complex dynamics at play. Rising interest rates can lead to a stronger currency, potentially weighing on commodity prices, particularly for those denominated in that currency. Additionally, higher borrowing costs can affect the cost of production and transportation, which may impact commodity prices differently across various sectors.

To navigate investing in a rising interest rate environment, investors should adopt a diversified portfolio strategy. Diversification helps spread risk across asset classes that may react differently to interest rate changes. In a rising interest rate environment, it may be prudent to consider increasing allocations to assets that historically perform well during such periods, such as inflation-protected bonds or dividend-paying stocks.

In conclusion, understanding interest rates and their influences is crucial for investors seeking to navigate a rising interest rate environment successfully. By comprehending the fundamental factors that affect interest rates and their potential impact on different investment categories, investors can make informed decisions to capitalize on opportunities and manage potential risks.

II

Impact of Rising Interest Rates

5

Overview

Investing in a rising interest rate environment can have significant impacts on various aspects of the economy and financial markets. As interest rates increase, the cost of borrowing money for businesses and individuals also rises, which can have wide-ranging effects on investments, financial planning, and overall market dynamics. In this overview, we will explore the impact of rising interest rates across different investment avenues.

Firstly, one area that experiences a direct impact from rising interest rates is fixed-income securities, particularly bonds. When interest rates rise, newly issued bonds come with higher coupon rates, making existing bonds with lower yields less desirable. Consequently, the prices of existing bonds decrease, as investors demand a higher yield to compensate for the higher rates available in the market. This movement in bond prices can create challenges for fixed-income investors, especially for those who hold longer-term bonds with fixed interest rates. However, in a rising interest rate environment, investors can consider shorter-term bonds or bond funds that can better adjust to changing interest rates.

In the equity markets, rising interest rates can cause shifts in investor sentiment and valuation metrics. As interest rates increase, the cost of borrowing for businesses rises, impacting their profitability and potentially slowing down economic growth. This can lead to a decrease in stock prices as companies' earnings expectations might get revised downwards. Additionally, higher interest rates can make fixed-income investments more attractive compared to equities, leading some investors to shift their allocations away from stocks. However, it is important to note that stock performance and market reactions to interest rate movements are influenced by various other factors, such as inflation expectations, economic conditions, and industry-specific dynamics.

Real estate investments can also be affected by rising interest rates. One of the key determinants of real estate valuations is the availability and cost of financing. When interest rates rise, the cost of borrowing for real estate transactions increases, which can reduce demand for properties, especially in sectors sensitive to interest rate fluctuations, such as residential housing and commercial real estate development. Rising interest rates can also drive up mortgage rates for homebuyers, potentially reducing affordability and slowing down the housing market. However, other factors such as supply and demand dynamics, regional market conditions, and housing policy also play significant roles in determining real estate investment outcomes.

Another asset class that can feel the impact of rising interest rates is commodities. As interest rates increase, the carrying cost of holding commodities, which don't provide any yield or interest, becomes relatively higher. This can lead to a decrease in commodity prices as speculation in commodities declines. Furthermore, rising interest rates can strengthen the domestic currency, potentially leading to lower commodity prices, as commodities are often priced in US dollars. However, the impact on individual commodities can vary depending on supply-demand dynamics, geopolitical factors, and specific market trends.

Investors can mitigate the impact of rising interest rates by diversifying their portfolios across different asset classes. This diversification helps ensure that the negative effects of one investment are balanced out or potentially offset by positive effects on others. Additionally, maintaining a long-term investment approach and regularly reviewing and rebalancing portfolios can be crucial to navigating through different economic cycles, including rising interest rate environments.

It is essential for investors to keep a watchful eye on economic indicators, central bank actions, and market sentiment when considering the impact of rising interest rates on their investment strategies. Staying informed and seeking professional advice can help investors make informed decisions tailored to their risk tolerance, investment goals, and time horizons.

6

On Bonds and Bond Funds

The impact of rising interest rates on bonds and bond funds is a crucial concept to understand when investing in a rising interest rate environment. To grasp this topic effectively, it's essential to have a solid understanding of bonds and how they work.

Bonds are a type of fixed-income investment where an investor lends money to an entity, such as a government or a corporation, in exchange for regular interest payments and the return of the principal amount at maturity. The interest rate on a bond, also known as the coupon rate, is typically fixed at the time of issuance.

When interest rates rise, it means that the overall cost of borrowing money increases. As a result, new bonds that are issued have higher coupon rates to compensate for the higher interest rates prevailing in the market. This poses a challenge to existing bonds and bond funds because their fixed coupon rates become less attractive compared to newer bonds with higher rates.

The relationship between interest rates and bond prices is inverse. When interest rates rise, the value of existing bonds with lower coupon rates decreases, as investors can obtain higher yields by investing in new bonds with higher coupon rates. Conversely, when interest rates decline, existing bonds become more valuable because their fixed coupon rates are higher than the prevailing rates in the market.

Bond funds, also known as mutual funds or exchange-traded funds (ETFs), are investment vehicles that pool money from numerous investors to invest in a diversified portfolio of bonds. The impact of rising interest rates on bond funds is similar to that on individual bonds, but with some additional nuances.

As interest rates rise, the net asset value (NAV) of a bond fund, which represents the value of its portfolio per share, tends to decline. This is because the prices of the underlying bonds in the fund decrease, lowering the overall value of the fund's portfolio. When this happens, investors may experience a decrease in the value of their shares in the bond fund.

However, bond funds also have some advantages over individual bonds in a rising interest rate environment. Bond funds provide diversification, spreading risk across a broad range of bonds. This diversification can help mitigate the negative impact of rising interest rates on the overall performance of the fund. Additionally, bond funds offer liquidity, allowing investors to buy and sell shares on any business day, making it easier to adjust their portfolios in response to changing market conditions.

Investors in a rising interest rate environment should carefully evaluate their bond holdings and bond fund investments. They may consider taking the following steps:

1. Assess the maturity of individual bonds:

Longer-term bonds tend to be more sensitive to changes in interest rates, meaning their prices can fluctuate more significantly than shorter-term bonds. Investors may consider adjusting their bond portfolio towards shorter-term maturities to reduce exposure to interest rate risk.

2. Consider bond funds with shorter duration:

Duration is a measure of a bond's sensitivity to changes in interest rates. Bond funds with shorter duration typically experience smaller price declines when interest rates rise. Investors may opt for bond funds that have shorter average durations to mitigate potential losses.

3. Evaluate the bond fund's quality and credit risk:

Bonds issued by entities with strong credit ratings are less susceptible to default and can fare better during periods of rising interest rates. Investors should examine the credit quality of the bonds held in the fund's portfolio to ensure they align with their risk tolerance.

4. Stay informed and seek professional advice:

Keeping abreast of current market conditions and seeking guidance from financial advisors or investment professionals can help investors make informed decisions about their bond investments in a rising interest rate environment.

It's important to keep in mind that investing in bonds and bond funds carries inherent risks, and the impact of rising interest rates is just one factor to consider. Diversification, risk tolerance, investment goals, and time horizon are crucial elements to evaluate when constructing a well-rounded investment portfolio.

7

On Stocks and Stock Funds

In the world of investing, understanding the impact of rising interest rates on stocks and stock funds is crucial for making informed decisions. As interest rates rise, it can have various effects on both individual stocks and broader stock funds. Let's delve into the topic and explore the implications of investing in a rising interest rate environment.

1. Relationship between Interest Rates and Stock Prices:

Generally, rising interest rates have an inverse relationship with stock prices. This means that as interest rates increase, stock prices tend to decline. This relationship is mainly driven by three key factors:

a. Cost of Borrowing:

Rising interest rates make borrowing more expensive for companies, which can lead to higher costs for expansion, research, and development. Consequently, this can limit their growth potential and negatively impact their profitability, causing a decline in stock prices.

b. Attraction towards Fixed Income:

When interest rates rise, fixed-income investments (such as bonds and certificates of deposit) become more attractive to investors since they offer higher yields with lower risk compared to stocks. As a result, some investors may shift their funds from stocks to fixed income, which can put downward pressure on stock prices.

c. Discounted Cash Flows:

In financial valuation models, the present value of future cash flows is determined by a discount rate. Rising interest rates increase this discount rate, which decreases the present value of expected future cash flows. Consequently, this can lead to a reduction in stock prices.

2. Impact on Different Sectors:

While rising interest rates generally affect stocks negatively, the degree of impact can vary across sectors. Some sectors are more sensitive to interest rate changes than others:

a. Financial Sector:

Financial institutions, such as banks and insurance companies, can benefit from rising interest rates. As interest rates increase, these institutions can earn higher interest income on loans and investments, which can boost their profitability. Consequently, this sector might experience positive effects on stock prices.

b. Utility and Real Estate Sectors:

These sectors, which often provide stable and consistent dividends, are more rate-sensitive. As interest rates rise, the cost of borrowing for utilities and real estate companies increases, potentially impacting their profit margins and stock performance.

c. Technology and Growth Companies:

Companies in the technology and growth sectors, which are often valued based on future earnings potential rather than current profitability, may be more sensitive to rising interest rates. As borrowing costs increase, the discount applied to future cash flows can negatively impact the valuation of these companies, leading to a potential decline in their stock prices.

3. Stock Funds and Diversification:

Investing in stock funds (such as mutual funds or exchange-traded funds) can provide diversification across various companies and sectors. Diversification can help mitigate some of the risks associated with rising interest rates. By investing in a diversified portfolio, the negative impact of rising rates on specific sectors or companies can be offset by the positive performance of others.

4. Timing and Long-term Perspective:

While the relationship between interest rates and stock prices is generally inverse, it is essential to recognize that other factors can influence the stock market's performance. Economic conditions, company-specific factors, and investor sentiment can all play significant roles. Investing should be approached with a long-term perspective, as short-term fluctuations caused by interest rate changes may not necessarily reflect the overall market trend.

In summary, rising interest rates can have a notable impact on both individual stocks and stock funds. Understanding the relationship between interest rates and stock prices, as well as the sector-specific effects, can assist investors in making informed decisions. Maintaining a diversified portfolio and focusing on long-term investment strategies are integral to navigating the potential challenges and opportunities presented by a rising interest rate environment.

8

On Real Estate Investment

Investing in real estate is a popular strategy for many individuals and companies. However, it's crucial to understand the potential impact of rising interest rates on real estate investments, especially in a rising interest rate environment. In this overview, we will explore the implications of higher interest rates on various aspects of real estate investment.

1. Financing Costs:

One of the primary concerns with rising interest rates is the increased cost of borrowing. When interest rates rise, the cost of obtaining financing for real estate investments also increases. This means that property buyers, developers, and investors may face higher mortgage rates, resulting in higher monthly payments and decreased affordability. These increased financing costs can affect the attractiveness of real estate investments and potentially reduce demand, especially for highly leveraged investments.

2. Property Values and Capitalization Rates:

Rising interest rates can have an impact on property values and capitalization rates. As interest rates increase, the expected return on real estate investments needs to compensate for the higher cost of financing. Consequently, higher interest rates can put downward pressure on property values, as investors may require higher yields to justify their investment. This can lead to a decrease in property prices or slower appreciation rates, particularly in areas with oversupply or weaker market fundamentals.

3. Rental Demand and Income:

Rental properties are a significant component of real estate investment. Rising interest rates can affect the demand for rental properties, as potential homebuyers may reconsider purchasing homes due to higher mortgage rates. Consequently, demand for rental properties may increase, leading to higher occupancy rates and potentially higher rental income. However, it's important to note that if rising interest rates also result in an economic slowdown or job losses, the demand for rental properties may weaken, impacting rental income.

4. Development Activities:

Rising interest rates can also impact real estate development activities. Higher borrowing costs can make financing new projects more expensive, resulting in a slowdown in real estate development. Developers may postpone or scale down their plans, reducing the supply of new properties. This reduction in supply could potentially support property values in the long run, but it could also lead to increased competition among developers and potential oversupply in certain markets.

5. Commercial Real Estate vs. Residential Real Estate:

The impact of rising interest rates can vary between commercial and residential real estate. Commercial real estate, particularly properties such as office buildings or shopping centers, may be more sensitive to interest rate changes. Higher interest rates can result in higher borrowing costs for businesses and potentially affect their ability to generate sufficient cash flow to cover lease payments. On the other hand, residential real estate may be less impacted, as people will always need a place to live. However, the potential decrease in affordability due to rising interest rates can affect the demand for residential properties, especially in regions with high price-to-income ratios.

6. Strategies for Investing in a Rising Interest Rate Environment:

Despite the challenges posed by rising interest rates, there are strategies that investors can employ in this environment. For instance, investors can focus on properties with stable income streams, such as multi-family apartments or commercial properties with long-term leases. Additionally, employing a conservative approach by considering lower leverage and longer-term fixed-rate financing options can mitigate the impact of rising interest rates on investment returns.

In conclusion, rising interest rates can impact various aspects of real estate investment. Higher financing costs, potential property value declines, and shifts in rental demand are some of the challenges that investors may face in a rising interest rate environment. Understanding these dynamics and employing appropriate strategies can help investors navigate this changing landscape and make informed investment decisions.

9

On Money Market Funds

In the context of investing in a rising interest rate environment, it is important to understand the impact of rising interest rates on money market funds. Money market funds are investment vehicles that aim to provide investors with low-risk, short-term investments while still generating a reasonable return.

When interest rates rise, it affects money market funds in multiple ways. Here is an extensive overview of the potential impacts:

1. Yields and Returns:

Rising interest rates generally lead to higher yields and returns on short-term fixed-income securities, such as Treasury bills, commercial paper, and certificates of deposit, which form the core holdings of money market funds. As a result, investors may experience higher yields and increased returns on their investments in money market funds.

2. Net Asset Value (NAV):

Money market funds have a target NAV of $1 per share. However, fluctuations in interest rates can impact the NAV. When rates rise, the yield on newly purchased, higher-yielding securities can surpass the average yield of existing securities in the fund, causing the fund's NAV to increase. Conversely, if interest rates fall, the lower yield on new securities may lead to a decline in the NAV.

3. Portfolio Composition:

In a rising interest rate environment, money market fund managers may adjust the fund's portfolio composition to take advantage of higher yields. They may increase allocations to higher-yielding securities, such as Treasury bills or commercial paper with slightly longer maturities. This proactive management aims to enhance returns for investors.

4. Risk vs. Reward:

While money market funds are generally considered low-risk investments, there are risks involved. In a rising interest rate environment, the risk of potential capital losses due to interest rate increases may slightly increase. However, these risks are typically minimal compared to other types of investments, such as stocks or longer-term bonds.

5. Investor Behavior:

Rising interest rates may also impact investor behavior. When rates rise, investors seeking higher returns may be inclined to shift their investments from money market funds to other investments offering potentially greater yields, such as bond funds or dividend-paying stocks. This shift may lead to a decrease in assets under management (AUM) for money market funds.

6. Investor Demand:

On the flip side, rising interest rates may also attract new investors seeking the stability and safety offered by money market funds. As yields rise, money market funds become more appealing relative to other low-risk investment options. This increased demand may counterbalance any potential outflows.

7. Regulatory Changes:

It is important to note that money market funds are subject to regulatory requirements, such as those imposed by the U.S. Securities and Exchange Commission (SEC). These regulations aim to ensure the stability and protection of investor assets. Changes in regulations may impact the structure and operation of money market funds, potentially affecting their behavior in a rising interest rate environment.

Overall, the impact of rising interest rates on money market funds is a complex interplay of yield changes, portfolio adjustments, investor behavior, and regulatory factors. While rising interest rates generally benefit money market funds in terms of higher yields and returns, investors should always monitor their investments and consult with financial professionals for personalized advice based on their specific financial goals and risk tolerance.

III

Strategies for Investing in a Rising Interest Rate Environment

10

Overview

In the context of investing, a rising interest rate environment refers to a situation where interest rates are increasing or are expected to increase in the future. Rising interest rates can have a significant impact on various aspects of the economy, including investments. As an investor, it becomes crucial to understand the strategies that can help navigate this environment and make informed decisions. Here is an extensive overview of strategies for investing in a rising interest rate environment:

1. Diversify your portfolio:

Diversifying your investments across different asset classes can help reduce the risk associated with rising interest rates. Consider allocating your funds across various sectors, such as stocks, bonds, real estate, commodities, and cash equivalents. By diversifying, you can minimize exposure to any single asset class and potentially offset losses in one area with gains in another.

2. Adjust bond holdings:

In a rising interest rate scenario, bond prices typically decline, as new bonds with higher interest rates become more attractive to investors. To mitigate potential losses, consider selling or reducing the duration of your long-term bonds and transitioning to shorter-term bonds or floating-rate bonds. Floating rate bonds are structured to adjust their interest rates according to changes in prevailing rates, providing a hedge against rising rates.

3. Invest in stocks of companies with low debt:

Companies with low levels of debt are generally better positioned to weather the impact of rising interest rates. Higher rates increase borrowing costs, negatively affecting companies with significant debt burdens. By focusing on companies with strong financial health and manageable debt levels, you can potentially reduce the risks associated with rising interest rates.

4. Consider dividend-paying stocks:

Dividend-paying stocks can be an attractive investment choice in a rising interest rate environment. As interest rates rise, the yield on fixed-income investments may increase, making them more appealing to investors seeking income. This could potentially lead to a decrease in demand for dividend-paying stocks, decreasing their prices. However, investing in quality dividend-paying stocks with a track record of consistently increasing dividends can provide a steady income stream and potential capital appreciation.

5. Explore alternative investments:

Alternative investments, such as real estate investment trusts (REITs), infrastructure funds, or commodities, often have a low correlation with traditional asset classes and can serve as a hedge against rising interest rates. These investments tend to be less sensitive to interest rate fluctuations and can provide potential diversification benefits to your portfolio.

6. Stay informed and adjust your strategy accordingly:

Keep a close eye on economic indicators, central bank policies, and market trends that influence interest rates. Regularly review and reassess your investment strategy to ensure that it aligns with the prevailing economic and market conditions. Seek expert advice or consult with a financial advisor to stay informed and make well-informed investment decisions.

7. Maintain a long-term perspective:

While rising interest rates may introduce short-term volatility and challenges, it is important to maintain a long-term perspective when investing. Historically, markets have experienced periods of rising interest rates, and investors who stayed focused on their long-term goals and resisted the temptation to make knee-jerk reactions often reaped the benefits. Patience, discipline, and a well-diversified portfolio can help navigate the challenges posed by rising interest rates.

Remember, investing involves risks, and strategies should be tailored to individual financial goals, risk tolerance, and investment horizon. It is advisable to thoroughly research and understand the potential risks and rewards of any investment strategy before making any investment decisions.

11

Diversification

Investing in a rising interest rate environment requires careful consideration and adaptation to changing market conditions. One significant strategy for managing investments in this scenario is diversification. Diversification involves allocating investments across a range of asset classes, industry sectors, geographic regions, and investment products. By spreading investments across different areas, investors can limit their exposure to risks associated with rising interest rates while aiming to maximize returns.

Here is an extensive overview of diversification strategies for investing in a rising interest rate environment:

1. Asset Allocation:

Investors can diversify their portfolio by allocating assets across different classes such as stocks, bonds, real estate, commodities, and cash equivalents. Stocks tend to perform better in a rising interest rate environment, as companies may experience increased profits due to economic growth. Bonds, on the other hand, may see a decline in value as interest rates rise, so it is essential to balance the allocation based on individual risk tolerance.

2. Bond selection:

Within the fixed-income asset class, selecting bonds with shorter maturities can reduce the impact of rising interest rates. Shorter-term bonds have less sensitivity to interest rate movements compared to longer-term bonds. Investors may also consider investing in inflation-protected securities (TIPS) or floating-rate bonds that can mitigate the negative effects of rising interest rates.

3. Sector Diversification:

Another aspect of diversification involves spreading investments across different industry sectors. While rising interest rates impact the overall economy, some sectors may be more affected than others. Analyzing historical trends and market research can help identify sectors that tend to perform well in rising-rate environments, such as financial services, energy, or technology.

4. Geographic Diversification:

Investing in diverse geographic regions can also mitigate risks associated with rising interest rates. Different countries or regions may experience varying interest rate policies and economic conditions. By investing globally, investors can benefit from different interest rate cycles and potentially enhance returns.

5. Alternative Investments:

In addition to traditional asset classes, investors may also consider allocating a portion of their portfolio to alternative investments, such as hedge funds, private equities, or real estate investment trusts (REITs). These alternatives typically exhibit a lower correlation to traditional markets and may provide additional diversification benefits.

6. Risk Management:

Implementing risk management strategies is crucial when investing in a rising interest rate environment. Setting stop-loss orders, regularly rebalancing the portfolio, and establishing clear investment objectives can help manage risk exposure and prevent significant losses.

7. Active Management:

Engaging in active management, either through self-directed investing or with the assistance of a professional fund manager or financial advisor, can allow for better monitoring and adjustment of investments based on changing market conditions. Regularly reviewing the portfolio and making necessary adjustments can ensure the diversification strategy remains aligned with investment goals.

It is important to note that diversification does not guarantee profits or protect against losses. Investors should carefully assess their risk tolerance, review their investment objectives, and consult with a financial advisor to tailor their diversification strategy to their specific needs and circumstances.

12

Short-Term Bonds

In the realm of investing, the interest rate environment plays a crucial role in determining the overall return on investment. A rising interest rate environment refers to a scenario where interest rates are expected to increase over time. This shift can impact various investment strategies, including those involving short-term bonds. In this overview, we will explore the subject of investing in short-term bonds, specifically in a rising interest rate environment, providing a simple yet extensive understanding of the strategies that can be employed.

1. Understanding Short-Term Bonds:

Short-term bonds are debt instruments issued by governments, municipalities, corporations, or other entities with a maturity period of typically one to five years. They are considered less exposed to interest rate fluctuations compared to long-term bonds, as they have shorter durations. This characteristic makes short-term bonds an attractive investment option to consider during a rising interest rate environment.

2. Focus on Yield and Coupon Payments:

When investing in short-term bonds in a rising interest rate environment, investors should focus on the yield and coupon payments offered by these bonds. Higher yields may be necessary to compensate for potential losses resulting from the interest rate increase. Monitoring changes in yields and assessing the overall reliability and creditworthiness of the issuer becomes crucial.

3. Laddering Strategy:

A commonly employed strategy in a rising interest rate environment is bond laddering. This approach involves spreading investments across multiple short-term bonds with staggered maturity dates. By doing so, investors can mitigate the impact of rising interest rates on their portfolios. As some bonds mature, the proceeds can be reinvested into new bonds with higher yields, capturing the increased interest rates.

4. Floating Rate Notes:

Floating rate notes (FRNs) are another suitable investment option during a rising interest rate environment. These bonds have adjustable interest rates, which are periodically reset according to prevailing market rates. Investing in FRNs allows investors to benefit from rising interest rates, as the coupons are adjusted accordingly.

5. Diversification:

Diversification is a fundamental principle in investing and applies to short-term bond portfolios as well. By diversifying across issuers, sectors, and credit ratings, investors can spread risks and potentially enhance their returns. Diversification ensures that the impact of any adverse interest rate movement on a single bond is limited.

6. Active Management:

Active management refers to the practice of actively monitoring and adjusting the composition of a portfolio based on market conditions. In a rising interest rate environment, active management becomes essential. An astute investor will continuously assess the interest rate trends, economic indicators, and credit rating changes to make informed decisions.

7. Consider Bond Funds:

Investors looking for broader exposure to short-term bonds while enjoying the benefits of professional management may consider investing in mutual funds or exchange-traded funds (ETFs) that focus on this asset class. Bond funds typically have a team of experienced managers who actively choose and manage a diversified portfolio of short-term bonds, responding to changes in interest rate conditions with expertise.

8. Risk Assessment and Professional Guidance:

Investing in short-term bonds or any other investment asset requires a thorough evaluation of the risks involved, based on an individual's financial goals, risk appetite, and investment horizon. Seeking advice from a financial advisor or investment professional with expertise in short-term bond investments can offer valuable insights, guidance, and tailored strategies based on personal circumstances.

Conclusion:

Investing in short-term bonds in a rising interest rate environment requires an understanding of the impact of interest rate changes and the implementation of suitable strategies. By focusing on yield, employing a laddering approach, considering floating rate notes, diversifying, actively managing the portfolio, and seeking professional guidance, investors can navigate the challenges and potentially capitalize on the opportunities presented by a rising interest rate environment.

13

Floating Rate Bonds

In the context of investing in a rising interest rate environment, strategies such as investing in floating-rate bonds can be helpful in managing the impact of interest rate changes on investment portfolios. Floating rate bonds, also known as adjustable or variable rate bonds, are debt securities that have coupon rates that adjust according to changes in a reference interest rate, such as the LIBOR or the U.S. Treasury rate.

Here is an extensive overview of strategies for investing in floating-rate bonds in a rising interest-rate environment:

1. Understanding the Relationship:

It is crucial to comprehend the inverse relationship between interest rates and bond prices. When interest rates rise, bond prices generally fall, and vice versa. This understanding sets the foundation for strategies to manage the impact of rising rates on investment portfolios.

2. Utilizing Floating Rate Bonds:

Floating rate bonds offer a unique advantage in a rising rate environment as their interest rates adjust periodically. This adjustment helps protect investors from a potential decrease in the bond's market value caused by increasing interest rates. Investing in floating-rate bonds can provide a hedge against rising rates, as their coupon payments will increase with rising rates.

3. Diversification:

As with any investment strategy, diversification is key. Investors should consider holding a diversified portfolio of bonds, including both fixed and floating-rate bonds, to spread risk and potentially mitigate the impact of rising interest rates. By combining different types of bonds, an investor can achieve a balanced approach that minimizes exposure to interest rate risk.

4. Understanding Credit Quality:

When investing in floating-rate bonds or any fixed-income instrument, it is crucial to evaluate the credit quality of the issuer. Assessing the creditworthiness of issuers helps gauge the level of risk associated with the investment. Higher-quality issuers typically offer more stability, while lower-quality issuers may provide higher yields but come with increased credit risk.

5. Active Portfolio Management:

In a rising interest rate environment, it is essential to actively manage investment portfolios. Strategies may involve adjusting the allocation between fixed and floating-rate bonds based on interest rate expectations and market conditions. Regular portfolio reviews and rebalancing should be undertaken to ensure that the portfolio remains aligned with investment goals and risk tolerance.

6. Consider Inflation Protection:

Rising interest rates often coincide with increasing inflation. Inflation protection bonds, such as Treasury Inflation-Protected Securities (TIPS), can be considered as part of an overall investment strategy to safeguard against the eroding effects of inflation.

7. Monitoring Economic Indicators:

Keeping a close eye on key economic indicators, such as central bank announcements, inflation rates, and GDP growth, can provide valuable insights into potential interest rate movements. Staying informed about macroeconomic trends can aid investors in making informed decisions and adjusting their strategies accordingly.

8. Consult with Financial Professionals:

Investing in a rising interest rate environment can be complex and challenging. Seeking advice from financial professionals, such as financial advisors or investment managers, can help investors navigate the complexities and implement suitable strategies based on their specific financial goals and risk tolerances.

Remember, investing in bonds, including floating rate bonds, carries risks, and past performance is not indicative of future results. Adequate research, risk assessment, and understanding of market dynamics are essential for successful investing in any environment, particularly in a rising interest rate scenario.

14

Dividend-Paying Stocks

Investing in a rising interest rate environment presents unique challenges for investors. As interest rates increase, the value of fixed-income investments, such as bonds, tends to decline. However, there are certain strategies that can be implemented to mitigate the potential negative impact of rising interest rates on investment portfolios.

One popular strategy in this context is investing in dividend-paying stocks. Dividend stocks are shares of companies that regularly distribute a portion of their profits to shareholders in the form of dividends. These stocks typically provide a steady income stream, making them an attractive option for investors seeking alternatives to fixed-income investments.

Here are some key strategies to consider when investing in dividend-paying stocks in a rising interest-rate environment:

1. Focus on Quality:

In times of rising interest rates, it is crucial to prioritize quality companies that have a stable track record of paying and growing dividends. Look for established companies with strong fundamentals, consistent earnings history, and sustainable dividend growth prospects.

2. Dividend Yield and Growth:

Pay attention to the dividend yield of the stocks you are considering. The dividend yield is the annual dividend payment divided by the stock price. Look for stocks with attractive dividend yields relative to their peers and historical averages. Additionally, companies that have a history of consistently increasing dividends may be better positioned to weather rising interest rates.

3. Sector Analysis:

Analyze different sectors to identify industries that have historically performed well in rising interest rate environments. Certain sectors, such as utilities, consumer staples, and healthcare, are often considered defensive sectors, as they tend to generate stable cash flows and offer reliable dividends.

4. Diversification:

Maintain a well-diversified portfolio by investing in dividend stocks from various sectors. This reduces concentration risk and helps spread potential risks associated with rising interest rates in a balanced manner.

5. Cash Flow Stability:

Consider companies with stable cash flows and sustainable business models. Companies with predictable revenue streams that are less sensitive to interest rate fluctuations are often better positioned to maintain dividends in a rising rate environment.

6. Dividend Reinvestment:

Reinvesting dividends can significantly enhance long-term returns. Consider setting up a dividend reinvestment plan (DRIP) that automatically reinvests dividends back into additional shares of the same stock, allowing compounded growth over time.

7. Active Management:

Consider actively managed dividend-focused funds or, alternatively, build your own dividend portfolio with individual stocks. Active management can help navigate market fluctuations and adjust holdings as interest rate cycles change.

8. Monitor Interest Rate Trends:

Stay informed about changes in interest rates and macroeconomic indicators that influence them. Central bank announcements, inflation outlook, and economic indicators can provide valuable insights into potential shifts in interest rate environments.

As with any investment strategy, it is crucial to conduct thorough research, understand your risk tolerance, and consider seeking advice from financial professionals before making any investment decisions. By implementing these strategies, investors can position themselves more effectively in a rising interest rate environment when investing in dividend-paying stocks.

15

Real Estate Investment Trusts (REITs)

Investing in real estate investment trusts (REITs) in a rising interest rate environment requires careful consideration and a strategic approach. A rising interest rate environment is characterized by an upward trend in interest rates set by central banks, leading to increased borrowing costs for businesses and individuals. This shift can have a significant impact on REITs as they rely on borrowing to fund their real estate investments.

Here is an extensive overview of strategies that can be employed when investing in REITs during a rising interest rate environment:

1. Focus on quality assets:

Investing in REITs with high-quality properties and a diversified portfolio can help mitigate risks during a rising interest rate environment. Look for REITs that own properties in strong markets and sectors with stable demand, such as healthcare, industrial, or multi-family residential.

2. Study interest rate sensitivity:

Evaluate the interest rate sensitivity of different REITs before making investment decisions. REITs that have long-term fixed-rate debt or shorter lease terms may be less sensitive to interest rate fluctuations compared to those with variable-rate debt or longer lease terms.

3. Analyze debt management:

Assess the REIT's debt levels, interest rate terms, and maturity dates. REITs with manageable debt levels and the ability to refinance at favorable rates may be better positioned to withstand increasing interest rates.

4. Seek REITs with interest rate hedges:

Some REITs utilize interest rate hedges or derivatives to protect against rising interest rates. These instruments can help offset potential interest rate risks, providing stability to the REIT's cash flows and dividends.

5. Consider floating rate REITs:

Floating rate REITs are a specialized type of REIT that invests in adjustable-rate mortgages or securities with interest rate resets. These REITs may benefit from rising interest rates as their income adjusts alongside these rate increases.

6. Evaluate management's actions:

Research and analyze the management team's strategy and track record in previous rising interest rate environments. Look for management teams that have successfully navigated challenging interest rate cycles and have implemented appropriate risk management measures.

7. Monitor market conditions and economic indicators:

Stay informed about relevant market conditions and economic indicators that can influence interest rates. This knowledge can help you make informed decisions and adjust your investment strategy accordingly.

8. Diversify your portfolio:

As with any investment strategy, diversification is crucial. Consider including a mix of various types of REITs, such as retail, office, residential, and healthcare, to spread risk and take advantage of opportunities in different sectors.

9. Long-term perspective:

Investing in REITs should be approached with a long-term perspective. Short-term interest rate fluctuations may cause market volatility, but a well-diversified REIT portfolio with stable fundamentals can generate attractive returns over time.

10. Consult with a financial advisor:

If you are not confident in your ability to navigate the complexities of investing in REITs during a rising interest rate environment, seek guidance from a qualified financial advisor. They can provide personalized advice based on your financial goals, risk tolerance, and market conditions.

Remember, investing in REITs always carries inherent risks. It is essential to conduct thorough research, stay informed, and carefully consider your investment objectives and risk tolerance before making any investment decisions.

16

High Yield Bonds

Investing in a rising interest rate environment entails considering various strategies to maximize returns and mitigate risks. In this context, high-yield bonds, also known as junk bonds, have gained prominence among investors. In this overview, we will explore the strategies for investing in high-yield bonds in such an environment, outlining their characteristics, advantages, and potential risks.

High-yield bonds are fixed-income instruments issued by corporations or governments with relatively lower credit ratings. These bonds offer higher yields compared to investment-grade bonds, compensating investors for the increased risk associated with the issuer's creditworthiness. Given the inverse relationship between bond prices and interest rates, high-yield bonds may be appealing in a rising interest rate environment. As interest rates rise, the value of existing bonds generally declines, which can negatively impact traditional fixed-income investments. On the contrary, high-yield bonds have shown a historical tendency to offer more protection against rising rates due to their higher yields.

When investing in high-yield bonds in a rising interest rate environment, there are several strategies to consider:

1. Active management:

Engaging in active management allows investors to actively select high-yield bonds based on their analysis of credit quality, market conditions, and interest rate expectations. Active managers seek to generate alpha by identifying undervalued securities and avoiding potential defaults. This strategy requires expertise and thorough research.

2. Diversification:

Diversifying your high-yield bond portfolio across various sectors, industries, and issuers helps reduce the impact of defaults and issuer-specific risks. By spreading investments across a range of high-yield bonds, investors can minimize exposure to any particular issuer or industry, thus enhancing risk management.

3. Sector rotation:

Monitoring and rotating investments across different sectors can provide opportunities for higher returns. Certain sectors may be more resilient to rising interest rates, while others may face challenges. By assessing sector-specific fundamentals and interest rate sensitivity, investors can adjust their holdings accordingly.

4. Duration management:

Duration refers to the sensitivity of a bond's price to changes in interest rates. In a rising rate environment, shorter-duration high-yield bonds may be less impacted compared to those with longer durations. Managing the average duration of a high-yield bond portfolio can help to limit potential losses stemming from rising rates.

5. Research and credit analysis:

In-depth research and credit analysis are vital when investing in high-yield bonds. Understanding the creditworthiness of issuers, evaluating their financial health, and assessing the potential risks they face is crucial to making informed investment decisions. Thorough analysis helps identify bonds with attractive risk-reward profiles.

Despite their potential advantages, investing in high-yield bonds in a rising interest rate environment carries certain risks:

1. Default risk:

High-yield bonds are typically issued by entities with lower credit ratings, increasing the probability of default. Economic downturns or adverse events can impact the ability of issuers to fulfill interest and principal payments, leading to potential losses for investors.

2. Liquidity risk:

High-yield bonds often have lower trading volumes compared to investment-grade bonds, making them less liquid. In times of market stress, it might be challenging to sell these bonds at desired prices, potentially resulting in reduced liquidity and increased transaction costs.

3. Interest rate risk:

While high-yield bonds have shown some resilience to rising interest rates, they are not immune to interest rate risk. If interest rates rise significantly, the value of high-yield bonds can still decline, impacting their market prices.

Investors considering high-yield bonds in a rising interest rate environment should carefully assess their risk tolerance, investment horizon, and overall portfolio objectives. Consulting with a financial advisor or professional with expertise in fixed-income investments can help you navigate the complexities and make informed decisions tailored to individual circumstances.

Please note that the information provided in this overview is for educational purposes only and should not be considered as financial advice. Individual investors should conduct their own research and consult with professionals before making investment decisions.

IV

Risks of Investing in a Rising Interest Rate Environment

17

Overview

Investing in a rising interest rate environment can be both rewarding and challenging. Interest rates have a significant impact on the overall economy and financial markets, thereby affecting various investment vehicles. To truly understand the risks involved in investing during such a period, it is crucial to have a clear overview of the subject.

1. Bond Market Risk:

The bond market is particularly sensitive to changes in interest rates. When rates rise, the prices of existing bonds decrease, resulting in potential capital losses for bondholders. This risk, known as interest rate risk, is especially prominent in long-term bonds with fixed interest rates. Investors holding such bonds may experience a decline in the market value of their investments, particularly if they need to sell before maturity.

2. Fixed-income Investments:

Along with bonds, other fixed-income investments, like certificates of deposit (CDs) and money market funds, are also impacted by rising interest rates. As new issuances offer higher rates, existing fixed-income investments become less attractive and may result in capital losses if sold before maturity.

3. Mortgage and Real Estate Market Risk:

In a rising interest rate environment, mortgages and other long-term loans become more expensive. This can decrease the demand for real estate, leading to potential declines in property prices. Investors reliant on income generated from rental properties may also face challenges in maintaining profitability as higher interest rates can affect rental demand and property valuations.

4. Equity Market Volatility:

Rising interest rates can introduce volatility into the equity markets. As borrowing costs increase, businesses may find it more challenging to expand or finance operations. Investors fearing the impact on corporate profitability may become more cautious, leading to market corrections or declines. Sectors sensitive to interest rates, such as utilities and consumer discretionary, may experience increased volatility during such periods.

5. Currency Risk:

When interest rates rise in a specific country, its currency often strengthens against other currencies. While this can benefit investors holding assets denominated in that currency, it may harm international investments or companies operating globally. Currency risk arises due to the potential devaluation of foreign currencies relative to the home currency, thereby impacting the returns on investments.

6. Inflation Risk:

Rising interest rates can be a response to increasing inflationary pressures. If interest rates fail to keep up with inflation, the purchasing power of investments may erode over time. Investors should be aware of this risk and consider investment vehicles that offer protection against inflation, such as inflation-adjusted bonds or certain commodities.

7. Portfolio Rebalancing:

In a rising interest rate environment, it becomes essential for investors to regularly review and rebalance their portfolios. As different asset classes are affected in distinct ways, a well-diversified portfolio may help mitigate risks. Rebalancing involves adjusting the allocation of investments to maintain the desired risk and return profile.

To successfully navigate the risks associated with investing in a rising interest rate environment, it is advisable to assess individual investment goals, risk tolerance, and time horizons. Seeking advice from financial professionals and staying informed about market dynamics is vital for making informed investment decisions.

18

Interest Rate Risk

Investing in a rising interest rate environment comes with its own set of risks, known as interest rate risk. Interest rate risk refers to the potential for changes in interest rates to negatively impact the value of an investment portfolio. When interest rates rise, there are several key areas of concern for investors to be aware of:

1. Bond Prices:

When interest rates increase, the prices of existing bonds tend to decrease. This is because newly issued bonds will offer higher interest rates, making older bonds with lower rates less attractive to investors. As a result, investors may experience losses if they need to sell their bonds before maturity. This risk is especially relevant for fixed-income investments like government and corporate bonds.

2. Dividend Yield:

Rising interest rates can impact the dividend yield of certain investments, particularly dividend-paying stocks. As interest rates increase, investors may prefer to invest in fixed-income securities instead of stocks, which could lead to a decrease in demand for dividend-paying stocks. Consequently, the prices of these stocks may decline, potentially resulting in a lower dividend yield.

3. Real Estate Market:

The real estate market can also be affected by rising interest rates. Higher interest rates make borrowing more expensive, which can slow down the housing market. Additionally, increased mortgage rates may discourage potential homebuyers, leading to a decrease in demand and potentially lower property values.

4. Credit Risks:

Rising interest rates can increase the cost of borrowing for individuals, businesses, and governments. If borrowers have difficulty paying higher interest expenses, it may lead to higher default rates and credit risks. This risk can affect investments tied to corporate bonds, loans, and certain types of debt-focused investments.

5. Equity Market Volatility:

In a rising interest rate environment, the equity market may experience increased volatility. Investors may become more cautious and reevaluate their investment strategies. Market volatility can lead to fluctuations in stock prices, which may impact the overall value of an investment portfolio.

To mitigate the risks associated with investing in a rising interest rate environment, investors can employ several strategies:

1. Diversification:

Spreading investments across different asset classes can help reduce exposure to interest rate risk. Diversifying a portfolio can include allocating investments to fixed-income assets, equities, real estate, and alternative investments.

2. Shorter Duration:

Investing in bonds with shorter durations can decrease interest rate risk. Shorter-term bonds are less sensitive to interest rate changes, allowing investors to reinvest at higher rates more quickly.

3. Active Monitoring:

Staying informed and actively monitoring market trends is crucial in managing interest rate risk. Keeping track of economic indicators, central bank decisions, and other relevant news can help investors make informed decisions.

4. Seek Professional Advice:

Consulting with a financial advisor can provide valuable insights and guidance for navigating the risks associated with a rising interest rate environment. A knowledgeable advisor can help develop personalized strategies based on an individual's risk tolerance, investment goals, and time horizon.

While investing in a rising interest rate environment carries inherent risks, being aware of these risks and adopting appropriate investment strategies can position investors to make informed decisions aimed at minimizing losses and maximizing returns.

19

Credit Risk

In the subject of investing in a rising interest rate environment, understanding the risks associated with credit becomes paramount. Credit risk refers to the potential for a borrower, such as a government, corporation, or individual, to default on their debt obligations. It becomes a particularly significant concern in an environment where interest rates are rising.

When interest rates increase, borrowing costs also rise. This can negatively impact the ability of businesses and individuals to fulfill their debt obligations, increasing the likelihood of default. As a result, investors who hold debt instruments issued by these borrowers may face potential losses.

Here is an extensive overview of the risks of investing in a rising interest rate environment with credit risk in mind:

1. Increased Borrowing Costs:

Rising interest rates lead to higher borrowing costs for businesses. This can affect their profitability and cash flow, making it more challenging for them to repay their debts. As a result, the likelihood of credit defaults increases.

2. Declining Bond Prices:

When interest rates rise, the prices of existing bonds tend to fall. This inverse relationship exists because new bonds issued at higher interest rates become more attractive to investors, reducing the demand for existing bonds with lower coupon rates. Therefore, if an investor needs to sell their bonds before maturity, they may incur losses due to declining bond prices.

3. Downgraded Credit Ratings:

In a rising interest rate environment, with higher borrowing costs and potential default risks, credit rating agencies may downgrade the credit ratings of borrowers. A lower credit rating means higher credit risk, and consequently, investors may demand higher yields to compensate for the increased risk.

4. Limited Availability of Credit:

When interest rates rise, lenders may become more cautious with their lending practices, increasing the creditworthiness standards for borrowers. This can lead to a reduction in the availability of credit, making it harder for companies to finance their operations and investments. This limited access to credit can negatively impact their ability to meet debt obligations.

5. Industry and Sector Vulnerabilities:

Certain industries or sectors are more susceptible to credit risk in a rising interest rate environment. For example, sectors that rely heavily on debt financing, such as real estate or utilities, may face higher risks due to their significant debt exposure.

6. Impact on Fixed-Income Investments:

Investors holding fixed-income investments, such as corporate bonds or government bonds, are exposed to credit risk. When interest rates rise, the creditworthiness of the issuer becomes even more critical. In the worst-case scenario, a bond issuer may default on its payment obligations, resulting in principal and interest loss for investors.

7. Impact on Banking Sector:

Rising interest rates can pose challenges to financial institutions. Banks often face credit risk through their lending activities and holdings of fixed-income investments. Higher default rates or declining bond values can negatively affect a bank's balance sheet, profitability, and overall stability.

To mitigate the risks associated with credit in a rising interest rate environment, investors can:

1. Diversify their portfolio:

By spreading investments across various assets, sectors, and credit ratings, investors can reduce their exposure to individual credit risks.

2. Research and analyze:

Thoroughly assess the creditworthiness and financial health of potential borrowers before investing. Review credit ratings, financial statements, and industry trends to gauge their ability to repay debt obligations.

3. Monitor interest rate trends:

Stay informed about interest rate movements and the potential impact on different sectors and markets. This can help investors adjust their strategies accordingly.

4. Seek professional advice:

Consult with financial advisors or experts who can provide guidance and recommendations tailored to individual investment objectives and risk tolerance.

In summary, investing in a rising interest rate environment carries inherent risks, particularly related to credit risk. By understanding these risks and implementing risk management strategies, investors can enhance their chances of navigating the challenges posed by fluctuating interest rates and the potential for credit defaults.

20

Inflation Risk

Investing in a rising interest rate environment can be a lucrative opportunity, but it also comes with its fair share of risks. One of the significant risks associated with this type of investment is inflation risk. Inflation risk refers to the potential loss of purchasing power due to the rising prices of goods and services.

When interest rates rise, it usually signifies that the economy is growing and that the central banks are attempting to control inflation. However, this can have a direct impact on the value of investments. Here's an extensive overview of the inflation risk in the context of investing in a rising interest rate environment:

1. Definition of inflation risk:

Inflation risk is the possibility that the purchasing power of your investment declines as the overall level of prices increase. In other words, it means that your investment returns may not keep up with the rising cost of goods and services, leading to a decrease in real value over time.

2. Impact on fixed-income investments:

Fixed-income investments like bonds are particularly vulnerable to inflation risk. When interest rates rise, the value of existing bonds with lower rates becomes less desirable. Investors may demand higher interest-paying bonds, leading to a decrease in the value of older bonds. This negatively affects the bond market, resulting in potential losses for investors holding fixed-income securities.

3. Impact on equity investments:

Rising interest rates can influence various sectors in the equity market differently. Some sectors, such as financial institutions, may benefit from higher interest rates due to increased profit margins. On the other hand, sectors sensitive to interest rates, like utilities, real estate, and consumer staples, can face challenges. Higher borrowing costs can impact their profitability and, subsequently, their stock prices. Inflation-eroding consumer purchasing power may also impact overall corporate earnings and market sentiment.

4. Mitigating inflation risk:

Investors have several strategies to mitigate inflation risk. One common approach is to invest in assets that tend to outperform during inflationary periods, such as commodities, real estate, and stocks of companies known for their ability to pass on increased costs to consumers. Diversification across different asset classes can also help reduce the impact of inflation on a portfolio.

5. Analyzing inflation data:

To effectively manage inflation risk, investors must closely monitor inflation indicators such as the Consumer Price Index (CPI), Producer Price Index (PPI), and wage growth reports. These indicators offer insights into the current and expected future inflation rates, assisting investors in making informed decisions about their investment allocations.

6. Inflation-indexed securities:

Investors looking to protect against inflation risk can consider allocating a portion of their portfolio to inflation-indexed securities like Treasury Inflation-Protected Securities (TIPS). These bonds provide principal and interest adjustments based on changes in inflation rates, thus preserving the purchasing power of investors' capital.

7. Other considerations:

Inflation risk is just one of the many risk factors investors should consider. Market volatility, interest rate fluctuations, geopolitical uncertainties, and other economic factors also play crucial roles in shaping investment outcomes. It's important to maintain a diversified portfolio, conduct thorough research, and seek professional advice when investing in a rising interest rate environment.

In conclusion, investing in a rising interest rate environment carries the risk of inflation eroding the purchasing power of investments. Understanding and effectively managing inflation risk is essential for investors to protect their portfolios and achieve their long-term investment objectives.

V

Benefits of Investing in a Rising Interest Rate Environment

21

Overview

Investing in a rising interest rate environment can have several benefits for individuals and businesses who carefully analyze and adapt their investment strategies. In this overview, we will explore some of the potential advantages of investing in such an environment.

1. Higher Fixed Income Returns:

When interest rates rise, the yields on fixed-income securities, such as bonds and certificates of deposit (CDs), tend to increase. This means that investors who hold these types of assets can earn higher returns on their investments. Consequently, investing in bonds or fixed-income funds becomes more appealing, especially for those seeking stable income streams.

2. Favorable Returns on Cash and Savings Accounts:

Rising interest rates often lead to higher interest rates offered on savings accounts, money market accounts, and other cash-based investments. This allows individuals to earn a higher return on their cash holdings, making it more attractive to hold cash or invest in short-term assets during such periods.

3. Profitable Long-Term Bond Strategies:

Although rising interest rates can initially present challenges for bond investors, they can also provide opportunities for savvy investors who implement the right strategies. For instance, investing in shorter-term bonds or bond funds with lower durations can help mitigate the negative impact of rising rates. Additionally, as older bonds with lower interest rates mature, investors can reinvest those funds into newer bonds with higher interest rates, effectively capturing higher yields.

4. Potential Equity Value Appreciation:

Although the relationship between interest rates and stock prices is complex, rising interest rates can sometimes be seen as an indicator of a robust economy. This can lead to increased business earnings and potential stock market growth. Companies that generate strong profits in a rising interest rate environment may experience an increase in their stock prices, benefiting equity investors.

5. Diversification Opportunities:

Investing in a rising interest rate environment can encourage individuals to diversify their investment portfolios. Allocating assets across different classes, such as stocks, bonds, real estate, and commodities, can help mitigate risks and take advantage of different market conditions. By rebalancing their portfolios according to changing interest rate dynamics, investors can position themselves for better returns.

6. Higher Returns on Money Market Funds:

Money market funds typically invest in highly liquid and short-term debt securities. As interest rates increase, the rates offered on money market funds tend to rise as well. This provides an opportunity for investors seeking stability and higher returns on their short-term investments.

7. Opportunities in Real Estate Investment Trusts (REITs):

Real Estate Investment Trusts, commonly known as REITs, can often benefit from rising interest rates. When rates increase, the cost of borrowing for individuals or businesses looking to purchase or develop real estate rises. This can lead to increased demand for rental properties and potentially higher rental prices, benefiting REITs and their investors.

It is essential to note that investing in any market environment carries risks, and a rising interest rate environment is no exception. Changes in interest rates can impact different asset classes differently, and each investor's situation is unique. Therefore, it is crucial to seek professional advice and conduct thorough research before making any investment decisions to ensure they align with your financial goals and risk tolerance.

22

Increased Returns on Fixed-Income Investments

Investing in a rising interest rate environment can offer several benefits, particularly when it comes to fixed-income investments. In this context, rising interest rates refer to an upward trend in the rates offered by financial institutions for borrowing money.

1. Increased Returns:

One of the primary benefits of investing in a rising interest rate environment is the potential for increased returns on fixed-income investments. When interest rates rise, newly issued fixed-income securities tend to offer higher yields compared to those issued earlier at lower rates. This means that investors who hold these newly issued securities can enjoy higher coupon payments, leading to increased returns on their investments.

2. Favorable Reinvestment Opportunities:

Rising interest rates can present favorable reinvestment opportunities for investors. As fixed-income investments, such as bonds or certificates of deposit (CDs), mature, investors can reinvest the proceeds at the new, higher rates. This allows them to capture the benefits of elevated rates and potentially generate higher income from their investments.

3. Preservation of Capital:

In a rising interest rate environment, fixed-income investments can act as a tool for preserving capital. When interest rates rise, the prices of existing fixed-income securities can decline. However, as fixed-income investments typically generate regular income streams, such as coupon payments, investors can still maintain stability and preserve the value of their investment portfolios.

4. Diversification Benefits:

Investing in fixed-income securities, such as bonds or treasury bills, can provide diversification benefits to an investment portfolio. With rising interest rates, the correlation between fixed-income securities and other asset classes, such as equities, may decrease. This means that fixed-income investments can act as a counterbalance to potential volatility in the equity markets.

5. Risk Mitigation:

In a rising interest rate environment, the risk of inflation also tends to increase. Fixed-income investments, particularly those with longer maturities, can serve as a hedge against inflation risk. As rates rise, fixed-income securities generally adjust their coupon payments according to the prevailing rates, thereby protecting investors from the eroding purchasing power associated with inflation.

6. Preservation of Income Streams:

For those investors who rely on fixed-income investments for regular income, a rising interest rate environment can help preserve their income streams. As rates increase, new fixed-income instruments offer higher yields, allowing investors to replace maturing lower-yielding investments with higher-yielding options. This ensures a steady income flow that matches or even surpasses the rate of inflation.

It is important to remember that while investing in a rising interest rate environment can provide these potential benefits, it is crucial to assess the individual risk tolerance, investment goals, and time horizon. Additionally, preferences for specific fixed-income securities, such as government bonds, corporate bonds, or municipal bonds, can vary based on individual circumstances. Seeking advice from a financial advisor or a professional investment manager can help align investment strategies with the vast array of possibilities presented by investing in a rising interest rate environment.

23

Potential for Capital Gains

Investing in a rising interest rate environment can present unique opportunities and benefits for investors. While rising interest rates may cause
initial concerns for some individuals, there are several potential benefits and
opportunities that can be capitalized on. One such benefit is the potential for
capital gains, which can lead to lucrative returns and increased wealth over
time.

1. Higher fixed-income yields

When interest rates rise, the yields on fixed-income securities such as
bonds and certificates of deposit (CDs) also tend to increase. This can be
advantageous for investors seeking stable and predictable income streams.
By investing in fixed-income assets with higher yields, investors can lock in
attractive rates that are not affected by further interest rate increases.

2. Inflation protection:

Rising interest rates are often accompanied by higher inflation rates. Inflation
erodes the purchasing power of money, leading to a decrease in the value of
savings. However, investing in assets that generate returns higher than the
inflation rate can help preserve and increase wealth. By carefully selecting

investments that are expected to outpace inflation, investors can effectively protect their purchasing power.

3. Enhanced return potential for equities:

Although rising interest rates can create short-term market volatility, they can also stimulate economic growth and corporate profitability. Companies often experience increased revenue and earnings during periods of economic expansion, which can positively impact stock prices. By investing in well-managed companies that are likely to benefit from the growing economy, investors can potentially realize capital gains as stock prices rise.

4. Attractive real estate opportunities:

In a rising interest rate environment, real estate markets can experience shifts in demand and supply dynamics. Higher interest rates can lead to reduced demand for mortgages and subsequently slow down housing markets. However, this situation can create advantageous opportunities for investors looking to purchase properties or invest in real estate investment trusts (REITs). As housing markets cool down, property prices may become more affordable, allowing investors to acquire assets at favorable prices with the potential for appreciation when the market rebounds.

5. Diversification and risk management:

Investing in a rising interest rate environment offers an opportunity to diversify one's portfolio. During periods of rising rates, different asset classes and sectors may react differently to changing economic conditions. By spreading investments across various asset classes, industries, and geographies, investors can mitigate risk and potentially enhance returns. Diversification allows for a better allocation of resources and minimizes exposure to any single economic event.

It is important to note that investing in a rising interest rate environment carries some risks, such as potential declines in bond prices and increased borrowing costs. Therefore, it is essential for investors to conduct thorough research, seek professional advice, and consider their risk tolerance and investment goals before making any investment decisions.

In conclusion, investing in a rising interest rate environment provides several potential benefits, including higher fixed-income yields, protection against inflation, enhanced return potential for equities, attractive real estate opportunities, and diversification benefits. By understanding these opportunities and conducting thorough analysis and research, investors can make informed decisions and potentially achieve capital gains in such an environment.

24

Opportunities for Diversification

Investing in a rising interest rate environment can present several benefits for investors who are well-prepared and knowledgeable. This overview will delve into the potential advantages of investing in such an environment, with a particular focus on opportunities for diversification.

1. Enhanced Yield Potential:

One of the primary benefits of investing in a rising interest rate environment is the potential for higher yields. As central banks increase interest rates, fixed-income securities such as bonds tend to offer higher coupon rates. This can generate greater income for investors who hold these securities, making them particularly attractive for income-oriented investors seeking greater yields.

2. Capital Preservation:

Rising interest rates can also help preserve the value of capital for investors with existing fixed-income holdings. When interest rates rise, the market value of pre-existing fixed-income securities may decrease. However, as these securities mature, investors can reinvest the proceeds at higher interest rates, thus capturing the benefit of the rising rates. Consequently, over time, investors may be better positioned to maintain the purchasing power of their capital.

3. Opportunities for Diversification:

A rising interest rate environment can create several opportunities for diversification within an investment portfolio. As interest rates increase, certain sectors such as financial services, real estate, and utilities tend to benefit. Investors can consider allocating their assets across these sectors to diversify risk and potentially reap the benefits of rising rates in different areas of the market.

4. Inflation Hedge:

Rising interest rates are often associated with inflationary pressures. Inflation erodes the purchasing power of money, and higher interest rates can mitigate this effect. Investments such as Treasury Inflation-Protected Securities (TIPS) offer explicit protection against inflation. Investing in TIPS or other inflation-protected assets during a rising interest rate environment can provide a hedge against the erosive effects of inflation on investment returns.

5. Flexibility for Active Investors:

Active investors who closely monitor economic indicators and interest rate movements can capitalize on the volatility caused by rising rates. As interest rates increase, market conditions may fluctuate, creating opportunities to buy undervalued assets or sell overpriced ones. Active investors can employ strategies such as duration management, tactical asset allocation, or sector rotation to potentially benefit from changing market dynamics.

6. Global Opportunities:

Rising interest rates are not exclusively limited to one region. Different countries and economies might experience varied interest rate trajectories based on their unique macroeconomic conditions. This provides investors with an opportunity to diversify across countries and regions, further expanding their investment options in a rising rate environment.

7. Rebalancing Possibilities:

A rising interest rate environment can prompt investors to reassess their asset allocation strategy. It may be an opportune time to rebalance and reallocate investments across asset classes. For example, as bonds become less attractive due to rising rates, investors can consider shifting towards equities or alternative investments, seeking potentially higher returns.

In conclusion, investing in a rising interest rate environment can offer several benefits, including enhanced yield potential, capital preservation, opportunities for diversification, an inflation hedge, flexibility for active investors, global opportunities, and the ability to rebalance portfolios. However, it's important to note that investing involves risks, and individual investors should carefully evaluate their goals and risk tolerance before making any investment decisions. Consulting with a financial advisor or investment professional may be beneficial to determine strategies that align with specific investment objectives.

25

Opportunity to Rebalance Portfolio

Investing in a rising interest rate environment provides several benefits, one of which is the opportunity to rebalance your portfolio. Rebalancing involves adjusting your investments to maintain a desired asset allocation, which can help you manage risk and optimize returns. In the context of rising interest rates, this strategy becomes even more crucial as it allows you to take advantage of market trends and reallocate your assets accordingly.

One benefit of rebalancing in a rising interest rate environment is the potential to increase overall portfolio returns. As interest rates rise, certain asset classes, such as bonds, tend to experience price declines. By reallocating some of your bond investments to other assets that may perform better in this environment, such as stocks or alternative investments, you can potentially generate higher returns.

Additionally, rebalancing in a rising interest rate environment allows you to manage risk more effectively. As interest rates increase, bond prices generally fall, leading to potential losses for bondholders. However, by rebalancing and reducing your exposure to bonds, you can mitigate the impact of these price declines and potentially minimize your overall portfolio risk.

Furthermore, rebalancing provides an opportunity to reassess your investment strategy and make adjustments to align with changing market conditions. In a rising interest rate environment, certain sectors or industries may benefit from higher interest rates, while others may face challenges. By rebalancing, you can reallocate your investments to sectors or industries that are poised to perform well in this environment, potentially enhancing your portfolio's performance.

Another advantage of rebalancing in a rising interest rate environment is the potential for income generation. As interest rates rise, certain fixed-income investments, such as bonds or money market funds, may offer higher yields. By adjusting your portfolio allocation to increase exposure to these income-generating assets, you can potentially benefit from the increased income stream.

Lastly, rebalancing provides an opportunity to take advantage of market volatility. In a rising interest rate environment, market volatility can increase, presenting opportunities for skilled investors to capitalize on market fluctuations. By rebalancing, you can take advantage of these market movements and potentially enhance your overall investment returns.

In summary, investing in a rising interest rate environment provides the opportunity to rebalance your portfolio, which offers numerous benefits. These include the potential to increase overall returns, manage risk effectively, align your investments with changing market conditions, generate income, and take advantage of market volatility. By staying proactive and adjusting your portfolio allocation in response to rising interest rates, you can optimize your investment strategy and potentially achieve your financial goals.

VI

Role of Central Banks in Interest Rates

26

Overview

The role of central banks in interest rates is a crucial aspect to consider when investing in a rising interest rate environment. Central banks are responsible for setting and managing monetary policy, which includes influencing interest rates. This can have significant implications for investors, as changes in interest rates directly impact the cost of borrowing and the return on investment.

In a rising interest rate environment, central banks typically aim to control inflation and maintain economic stability. This is achieved by increasing interest rates to encourage saving, limit borrowing, and reduce spending. Higher interest rates can also attract foreign capital, strengthen the currency, and control inflationary pressures. However, these actions can have several effects on investments:

1. Bonds and Fixed-Income Investments:

Rising interest rates can lead to a decline in the value of existing bonds and fixed-income investments. This happens because newly issued bonds with higher interest rates become more attractive to investors, reducing the demand for existing bonds. As a result, bond prices tend to decrease, which can lead to losses for bondholders.

2. Stocks and Equities:

Rising interest rates can impact stocks and equities in various ways. Firstly, the discount rate used to value future cash flows of companies increases, which can lower their present value and potentially decrease stock prices. Secondly, high interest rates can make borrowing more expensive, affecting companies that heavily rely on debt for growth. Lastly, rising interest rates can have a negative impact on consumer spending, which can result in reduced company revenues and lower stock prices.

3. Real Estate:

The real estate market is sensitive to interest rate changes. Higher interest rates mean increased mortgage rates, making homes less affordable for potential buyers. Consequently, the demand for real estate may decrease, causing property prices to stagnate or even decline. Additionally, rising interest rates can increase borrowing costs for real estate developers, potentially impacting their ability to invest in new projects.

4. Currencies:

Central banks' decisions on interest rates can have a significant impact on currency exchange rates. Higher interest rates typically attract foreign investors seeking higher returns. As a result, the demand for a country's currency increases, leading to appreciation. This appreciation can positively impact investments denominated in that currency, as the value of investments in foreign currencies increases.

5. Diversification and Risk Management:

In a rising interest rate environment, it becomes essential for investors to diversify their portfolios to mitigate the potential risks associated with interest rate fluctuations. A diversified portfolio can include a mix of asset classes, such as bonds, stocks, real estate, commodities, and currencies, which can help manage risk exposure and potentially minimize losses.

It is crucial for investors to closely monitor central bank policies and forecasts, as they provide insights into potential future interest rate changes. By staying informed, investors can adapt their investment strategies to maximize returns or minimize potential losses in a rising interest rate environment.

Overall, understanding the role of central banks in setting interest rates is fundamental for investors navigating a rising interest rate environment. By carefully considering the effects of interest rate changes on various investment options, diversifying portfolios, and staying informed about central bank policies, investors can make better-informed decisions to navigate these market conditions successfully.

27

Federal Reserve (US)

The role of central banks, specifically the Federal Reserve in the United States, in interest rates is a crucial aspect to consider when investing in a rising interest rate environment. In this overview, we will discuss the key factors related to the Federal Reserve's influence on interest rates and how it impacts investment decisions in such scenarios.

1. Federal Reserve's Monetary Policy:

The Federal Reserve is responsible for maintaining price stability and fostering sustainable economic growth in the United States. One of the primary tools used to achieve these goals is monetary policy, which encompasses various measures to regulate interest rates.

2. The Federal Funds Rate:

The Federal Reserve sets a target range for the federal funds rate, which is the interest rate at which banks lend to each other overnight to meet reserve requirements. This rate serves as a benchmark for many other interest rates in the economy and influences borrowing costs for businesses, individuals, and investors.

3. Open Market Operations:

The Federal Reserve utilizes open market operations to influence interest rates. Through the buying and selling of government securities (e.g., Treasury bonds), the Federal Reserve aims to adjust the supply of money in the banking system, thereby influencing short-term interest rates.

4. Impact on Bond Market:

Rising interest rates generally result in lower bond prices. When the Federal Reserve raises interest rates, bond yields tend to increase, reducing the attractiveness of existing bonds with lower yields. Consequently, investors may shift their investments towards cash or other assets with higher yields, impacting bond prices and the overall bond market.

5. Effects on Equity Markets:

Rising interest rates can also influence equity markets. As borrowing costs increase, companies may find it more expensive to finance their operations. This scenario might lead to decreased profitability and valuation multiples, potentially impacting stock prices. Additionally, rising interest rates may make fixed-income investments more appealing compared to equities for some investors.

6. Sectoral Impact:

Different sectors of the economy react differently to rising interest rates. For instance, sectors such as financial services may benefit from higher rates due to increased profit margins from lending activities. Conversely, sectors relying heavily on borrowing, such as real estate or highly indebted companies, might face challenges as their borrowing costs rise.

7. International Impact:

While the Federal Reserve's actions specifically target the United States, changes in interest rates can have spillover effects on global markets. Investor sentiment, capital flows, and exchange rates may be influenced by interest rate differentials between the U.S. and other countries, leading to potential implications for international investments.

8. Market Expectations and Reactions:

Investors closely monitor and may attempt to anticipate the Federal Reserve's actions to position their investments accordingly. Changes in interest rate expectations can affect market volatility, asset prices, and investor behavior. Consequently, investors must stay informed about economic indicators, central bank communications, and policy decisions to make well-informed investment decisions.

9. Diversification and Risk Management:

Investing in a rising interest rate environment requires careful assessment and diversification of one's portfolio. Diversifying investments across different asset classes, including fixed-income securities with varying maturities, equities, commodities, and currencies, can help mitigate risk associated with rising interest rates.

In conclusion, the role of the Federal Reserve in influencing interest rates has a significant impact on investment decisions, particularly in a rising interest rate environment. Understanding the central bank's monetary policy, the effects on bond and equity markets, sectoral implications, international influences, investor reactions, and the importance of diversification are essential elements for navigating investments in such circumstances.

28

European Central Bank (Europe)

The role of central banks in determining and influencing interest rates is of utmost importance in the global financial system. In Europe, the European Central Bank (ECB) plays a crucial role in setting interest rates for the Eurozone countries. Understanding the role of central banks, particularly the ECB, is essential for individuals and investors navigating the complexities of investing in a rising interest rate environment.

Central banks, including the ECB, have the primary objective of maintaining price stability and supporting sustainable economic growth. To achieve these goals, central banks utilize various monetary policy tools, with one of the most influential being the manipulation of interest rates.

In a rising interest rate environment, central banks typically employ contractionary monetary policy measures. The objective is to cool down the economy to prevent overheating, control inflation, and maintain price stability. Central banks achieve this by raising interest rates, making borrowing more expensive and subsequently curbing consumption and investment.

For the ECB, determining interest rates involves a comprehensive analysis of numerous economic indicators, including inflation rates, GDP growth, unemployment levels, and overall economic climate. The ECB's Governing

Council, composed of the Executive Board and the governors of national central banks within the Eurozone, deliberates and sets the main refinancing rate, which serves as a benchmark for other interest rates within the Eurozone.

Rising interest rates impact various aspects of the financial and investment landscape. It affects borrowing costs for individuals, businesses, and governments, leading to increased expenses for loans, mortgages, and other forms of credit. Investors who rely on debt financing may experience higher interest payments, potentially reducing their profitability.

In terms of asset classes, rising interest rates can have diverse effects. Bond prices typically move inversely to interest rates, meaning that as rates rise, bond prices tend to decline. This can lead to potential capital losses for investors holding bonds. Similarly, dividend-paying stocks may face downward pressure, as higher interest rates make fixed-income instruments more attractive to investors seeking income generation.

However, not all investments are negatively affected by rising interest rates. Certain assets, such as money market instruments, certificates of deposit, and high-yield savings accounts, may see increased returns as interest rates rise. Moreover, companies in cyclical sectors, such as financials and industrials, can sometimes benefit from a rising interest rate environment as it indicates a strong economy and increased business activity.

To navigate investing in a rising interest rate environment, individuals and investors should consider diversifying their portfolios. This involves allocating investments across various asset classes and sectors to mitigate risks associated with interest rate fluctuations. Additionally, staying informed about the ECB's monetary policy decisions, economic indicators, and global macroeconomic trends is crucial for anticipating and adapting to changes stemming from rising interest rates.

In conclusion, central banks, including the European Central Bank, play a pivotal role in determining interest rates, which have wide-ranging implications for individuals and investors. Understanding the mechanisms through which central banks influence interest rates, particularly in a rising rate environment, is essential for making informed investment decisions and managing the associated risks. Keeping a balanced and diversified portfolio, while staying informed about monetary policy decisions, can help investors navigate the challenges and opportunities presented by rising interest rates.

29

Bank of England (UK)

The role of central banks in determining interest rates is crucial in the realm of investing in a rising interest rate environment. In the case of the Bank of England (BoE) in the United Kingdom, its primary objective is to maintain price stability and support the overall economic growth and financial stability of the country. As such, the BoE utilizes various tools and strategies to influence interest rates and guide economic conditions.

One of the primary instruments used by the BoE is the setting of the Bank Rate, also known as the base rate or the interest rate at which it provides funds to commercial banks. The Bank Rate directly affects borrowing costs for banks, and consequently, influences the interest rates they offer to individuals and businesses. Therefore, when the BoE raises the Bank Rate, it generally leads to an increase in borrowing costs across the economy.

The decision to raise or lower the Bank Rate is based on several factors. The BoE's Monetary Policy Committee (MPC) assesses various economic indicators such as inflation rates, GDP growth, employment levels, and financial market conditions. If the MPC observes that inflation is above the target level set by the government, it may raise interest rates to curtail spending and reduce inflationary pressures. Conversely, if the economy is experiencing a downturn, the MPC could lower interest rates to stimulate borrowing, spending, and economic activity.

The impact of rising interest rates on investments in a rising interest rate environment depends on the specific investment vehicles involved. Fixed-income investments, such as bonds, tend to be negatively affected by rising interest rates. As the interest rates increase, the yield on new bonds rises, making existing bonds with lower yields less attractive to investors. This dynamic can lead to a decline in bond prices in the secondary market.

On the other hand, rising interest rates may benefit certain investments. For instance, savings accounts and other liquid cash instruments tend to yield higher returns as interest rates increase. This can be advantageous for individuals seeking to increase their savings or investors looking for safe and stable returns.

In the context of stock markets, the impact of rising interest rates can be mixed. Higher interest rates may increase borrowing costs for companies, potentially squeezing profit margins. This may result in a more cautious investor sentiment, which could lead to a decrease in stock prices. However, some industries, particularly financial institutions, may benefit from higher interest rates, as they tend to have higher profit margins when borrowing costs are elevated.

Furthermore, the BoE's interest rate decisions can have knock-on effects on currency exchange rates. Higher interest rates generally strengthen a currency as it attracts foreign investment and increases the returns on investments denominated in that currency. This can have implications for investors holding assets denominated in other currencies.

In summary, the role of the Bank of England in determining interest rates is pivotal in shaping the investment landscape in a rising interest rate environment. The Bank's decisions can have wide-ranging effects on various investment vehicles, such as bonds, stocks, and currencies. It is crucial for investors to stay informed about the BoE's monetary policy actions and consider the potential impacts on their investment portfolios.

30

Bank of Japan (Japan)

The role of central banks, such as the Bank of Japan (BoJ), in determining and influencing interest rates is crucial in understanding the impact on investments, particularly in a rising interest rate environment. This overview will provide a comprehensive understanding of the BoJ's role in setting interest rates and how it affects investment strategies in Japan.

The Bank of Japan, as the country's central bank, has the responsibility of maintaining price stability, ensuring financial system stability, and supporting economic growth. One of the primary tools they employ to achieve these objectives is the manipulation of interest rates. By altering certain interest rates, the BoJ aims to control the supply of money and credit in the economy, thereby influencing borrowing costs, consumption, and overall economic activity.

In a rising interest rate environment, central banks, including the BoJ, typically raise interest rates to curb inflationary pressures or to cool down an overheating economy. When interest rates increase, borrowing becomes more expensive, which can slow down investment and consumption. This can have a significant impact on various aspects of investing.

One of the key areas affected by rising interest rates is the bond market. As interest rates rise, the prices of existing bonds tend to fall. This is because newly issued bonds offer higher yields, making existing bonds with lower yields less attractive to investors. Consequently, investors may experience a decline in the value of their bond holdings, which can impact their investment portfolios.

Additionally, rising interest rates often have repercussions on stock markets. Higher interest rates tend to increase borrowing costs for businesses, which can impact their profitability and shareholder returns. As a result, investors may experience downward pressure on stock prices. However, this impact may vary across different sectors, as certain industries may be more sensitive to interest rate changes than others. For instance, sectors such as utilities and real estate investment trusts (REITs) tend to be more interest-rate-sensitive due to their capital-intensive nature and reliance on borrowing.

Furthermore, a rising interest rate environment can affect currency markets. Higher interest rates often increase the attractiveness of a country's currency, as it raises the return on investments denominated in that currency. As a result, the value of the currency may appreciate, impacting international investors and businesses involved in import and export activities.

Considering the specific context of Japan, the Bank of Japan has maintained a historically low interest rate policy for an extended period to combat deflation and encourage economic growth. With the prolonged low-interest rate environment, investors in Japan have become accustomed to the availability of cheap financing. However, if the BoJ were to shift towards a rising interest rate policy, it could have profound implications for investors in the country.

In an environment of rising interest rates, investors in Japan might need to reconsider their investment strategies. Higher borrowing costs could impact the profitability of businesses, leading to potential shifts in sector performance. For instance, sectors such as financials might benefit from rising interest rates due to their ability to generate higher interest income, while interest rate-sensitive sectors like real estate or utilities may face challenges.

Additionally, investors may need to reassess their bond portfolios. Rising interest rates often lead to lower bond prices, which can impact fixed-income investments. Investors may need to consider diversifying their portfolios and exploring alternatives to traditional bonds, such as shorter-duration bonds or adjustable-rate securities.

In conclusion, the role of central banks, such as the Bank of Japan, in determining and influencing interest rates is vital in shaping investment strategies, particularly in a rising interest rate environment. Investors should closely monitor the actions and policies of central banks, as their decisions can have profound effects on various asset classes, including bonds, stocks, and currencies. Understanding the relationship between central bank actions, interest rates, and investment performance is crucial for adapting to changing market conditions and optimizing investment strategies.

VII

Interest Rate Predictions and Forecasting

31

Overview

Investing in a rising interest rate environment requires careful consideration and understanding of interest rate predictions and forecasting. As interest rates play a crucial role in the economy and financial markets, accurately predicting and forecasting them is essential for investors to make informed decisions.

Interest rates, typically determined by central banks, have a significant impact on various aspects of the financial world. When interest rates rise, it affects borrowing costs, investment decisions, bond yields, and equity valuations. Therefore, investors need to gauge the future movement of interest rates to adjust their investment strategies accordingly.

To predict and forecast interest rate changes, analysts and investors employ various methods and tools. Some commonly used approaches include fundamental analysis, technical analysis, and market sentiment analysis.

Fundamental analysis involves examining economic indicators, such as inflation, gross domestic product (GDP) growth, employment figures, and fiscal policies, to assess the overall health of the economy and potential interest rate movements. For instance, if the economy is showing signs of strong growth and inflationary pressures, it may indicate a higher likelihood of interest rate hikes.

Technical analysis entails studying historical price and volume patterns in financial markets. Analysts analyze charts, trends, and patterns to identify potential interest rate signals. Technical indicators, such as moving averages and oscillators, are commonly used to predict interest rate direction based on past market behavior.

Market sentiment analysis involves considering the opinions and expectations of market participants, including investors, central bankers, and economists. By analyzing surveys, market reports, and expert opinions, investors can gain insights into the overall consensus regarding future interest rate movements.

Apart from these approaches, model-based forecasting techniques can also be employed. These models incorporate a range of variables and use statistical methods to predict future interest rate changes. Popular models include the Taylor rule, which relates interest rates to inflation and output gaps, and the yield curve model, which analyzes the relationship between short-term and long-term interest rates.

It is important to note that interest rate predictions and forecasting are inherently challenging and subject to uncertainties. Economic and geopolitical events, policy changes, and unexpected developments can influence interest rates in ways that are difficult to predict accurately. Therefore, investors should consider multiple sources of information and seek expert opinions to form a well-rounded view of the potential interest rate trajectory.

In conclusion, understanding interest rate predictions and forecasting is crucial for investors looking to navigate the challenges of investing in a rising interest rate environment. By utilizing fundamental analysis, technical analysis, market sentiment analysis, and model-based forecasting techniques, investors can make informed decisions regarding their investment strategies. Nonetheless, it is important to remain vigilant and flexible, as interest rate dynamics can be impacted by various unpredictable factors.

32

Economic Indicators

Investing in a rising interest rate environment requires an understanding of interest rate predictions and forecasting economic indicators. This overview will provide a simple yet comprehensive explanation of these concepts.

Interest rate predictions involve forecasting the direction and magnitude of changes in interest rates. These predictions are based on various economic indicators, which provide insights into the health and direction of the economy. By analyzing these indicators, investors can make informed decisions on how rising interest rates may impact their investment portfolios.

To forecast interest rates, economists and analysts consider a range of economic indicators, including:

1. Gross Domestic Product (GDP):

GDP measures the total value of goods and services produced within a country's borders. A strong GDP growth rate often suggests a robust economy and may lead to higher interest rates as central banks aim to cool down potential inflation.

2. Inflation Rate:

The inflation rate measures the change in the general level of prices for goods and services over time. Central banks usually raise interest rates to control inflation. Therefore, higher inflation rates may indicate a higher probability of interest rate hikes.

3. Unemployment Rate:

The unemployment rate reflects the percentage of the labor force that is unemployed. A low unemployment rate typically indicates a strong economy and may contribute to higher interest rates.

4. Consumer Price Index (CPI):

The CPI measures changes in the average prices of a basket of goods and services purchased by households. Rising CPI implies inflationary pressure, potentially leading to higher interest rates.

5. Central Bank Policies:

Observing the actions and statements of central banks, such as the Federal Reserve in the United States, can provide valuable insights into future interest rate movements. Central banks often use interest rate adjustments as a tool to manage economic conditions.

6. Market Expectations:

Analysts often consider market expectations derived from various sources, including interest rate futures contracts, to gauge market sentiment regarding future interest rate changes. These expectations can influence investor behavior and market dynamics.

In a rising interest rate environment, investors need to consider the potential impact on various asset classes. Higher interest rates can lead to increased borrowing costs, which may affect businesses and consumer spending. Additionally, rising rates can influence the valuation of stocks, bonds, and real estate investments.

To navigate this environment, investors can take a few key steps:

1. Diversify Portfolio:

Spreading investments across different asset classes can help mitigate risks associated with interest rate fluctuations. Diversification allows investors to benefit from the potential upside of certain investments while minimizing exposure to any single asset class.

2. Evaluate Fixed-Income Investments:

Rising interest rates can negatively impact the value of fixed-income investments, such as bonds. Investors should carefully evaluate their bond holdings, considering factors such as bond duration and interest rate sensitivity.

3. Monitor Industry Performance:

Certain industries, like financials, tend to perform better in a rising interest rate environment, while others, such as utilities, may face challenges. Keeping an eye on the performance of specific sectors can help identify investment opportunities or potential risks.

4. Stay Informed:

Continuously monitoring economic indicators and staying updated with the latest news and analysis is crucial for making informed investment decisions in a rising interest rate environment. Access to reliable financial sources and expert opinions can help shape investment strategies.

Investing in a rising interest rate environment requires a thorough under-standing of interest rate predictions, economic indicators, and their potential impacts on various investments. By keeping track of these factors and maintaining a diversified portfolio, investors can position themselves to make informed decisions and navigate changing market conditions.

33

Market Expectations

In investing, understanding the concept of interest rate predictions and forecasting market expectations is crucial, especially in a rising interest rate environment. Interest rates play a significant role in the economy and have a direct impact on various investment avenues like bonds, stocks, and real estate. Being able to predict and anticipate the direction of interest rates can help investors make informed decisions and optimize their portfolio returns. In this overview, we will explore the basics of interest rate predictions, the factors influencing them, and strategies for investing in a rising interest rate environment.

Interest rate predictions involve trying to forecast the future movements of interest rates, typically set by central banks in response to economic conditions. Central banks hike or reduce interest rates to control inflation, stimulate or cool down economic growth, and influence borrowing and lending rates across the economy. While it is highly challenging to accurately predict interest rate movements, investors, economists, and financial institutions analyze a variety of factors to assess future trends.

Market expectations play a crucial role in shaping interest rate predictions. Investors analyze various economic indicators, such as GDP growth, inflation rates, employment data, and consumer confidence, to gauge the overall health of an economy. Additionally, central bank speeches, policy statements, and minutes from meetings provide valuable insights into their intentions regarding interest rate changes. By evaluating these indicators and market sentiment, investors attempt to anticipate the future path of interest rates.

In a rising interest rate environment, where interest rates are expected to increase, investors need to adjust their investment strategies to mitigate potential risks and seize opportunities. Here are some key considerations and investment strategies to navigate this environment:

1. Bonds:

Rising interest rates can have a negative impact on bond prices. As interest rates increase, newer bonds with higher yields become available, reducing the attractiveness of existing lower-yielding bonds. Investors may consider diversifying their bond holdings by investing in shorter-term bonds that are less sensitive to interest rate changes. Additionally, considering bonds with built-in interest rate protection, such as inflation-linked bonds or floating-rate bonds, can provide some degree of insulation from rising rates.

2. Stocks:

A rising interest rate environment can lead to increased borrowing costs for companies, impacting their profitability and stock prices. Investors may focus on stocks of sectors that tend to perform well in such environments, such as financial institutions that benefit from higher interest rate spreads. Additionally, focusing on dividend-paying stocks can be advantageous as they provide income even if capital appreciation is limited.

3. Real Estate:

Rising interest rates can impact the affordability of mortgages, potentially slowing down the real estate market. Investors may consider shifting towards real estate investment trusts (REITs) that have a diversified portfolio of properties, including commercial, residential, or industrial. Additionally, investing in regions or markets with strong demand fundamentals can help withstand potential challenges caused by rising interest rates.

4. Cash and Cash Equivalents:

Holding a portion of your portfolio in cash or cash equivalents, such as money market funds, can provide flexibility and potential opportunities to invest in higher yielding assets once interest rates stabilize.

It is important to note that interest rate predictions and market expectations are subject to uncertainty and can be influenced by unexpected events or changes in economic conditions. Therefore, regularly monitoring economic indicators and staying informed about central bank decisions and policies is crucial for successful investing.

Ultimately, navigating a rising interest rate environment requires a well-diversified portfolio, careful analysis of individual investment options, and staying attuned to market developments. Consulting with a financial advisor or investment professional can also provide valuable guidance based on your specific investment goals and risk tolerance.

34

Central Bank Policies

Investing in a rising interest rate environment requires a careful analysis of interest rate predictions and the policies undertaken by central banks. Interest rates play a crucial role in the performance of various investment assets, including stocks, bonds, real estate, and commodities. As an investor, understanding the dynamics of interest rates and central bank policies can help you make more informed investment decisions.

Interest rate predictions involve forecasting the direction and magnitude of interest rate changes in the future. Several factors influence interest rates, including inflation, economic growth, monetary policy decisions, and market expectations. It is important to note that predicting interest rates accurately is challenging and subject to uncertainties, as they are influenced by multiple complex and interrelated factors.

Central banks, such as the Federal Reserve in the United States, the European Central Bank, or the Bank of England, have significant power over interest rates. These institutions use monetary policy tools to influence the economy by setting short-term interest rates and controlling the money supply. In a rising interest rate environment, central banks typically aim to curb inflation and control economic growth by increasing interest rates.

To forecast central bank policies, investors closely monitor economic indicators, listen to central bank statements, and evaluate the prevailing economic conditions. Key economic indicators might include inflation rates, GDP growth, employment data, and consumer sentiment. Central bank statements, press conferences, and minutes from policy meetings provide valuable insights into future policy decisions and interest rate expectations.

In a rising interest rate environment, several investment strategies can be considered:

1. Fixed-income investments:

Rising interest rates often lead to a decline in bond prices, as newer bonds offer higher yields. Investors need to be cautious when investing in long-term bonds, as they will be more sensitive to interest rate changes. Short-term bonds or bond funds that adjust their portfolio duration can be more suitable in such an environment.

2. Equities:

Rising interest rates can impact stock prices, especially for industries that are interest rate-sensitive, such as utilities or real estate. However, certain sectors, like financials, may benefit from higher interest rates, as their profitability can improve. Investors should diversify their equity portfolio across sectors to mitigate risks associated with rising interest rates.

3. Real estate:

Higher interest rates can affect the affordability of mortgages, potentially dampening demand for real estate. However, properties with stable rental income and long-term lease agreements may withstand interest rate increases better. Additionally, commercial real estate can benefit from rising rates, as it can reflect an expanding economy and increased business activity.

4. Commodities and currencies:

Rising interest rates can influence currency valuations and commodity prices. Currencies of countries with higher interest rates tend to strengthen against those with lower rates. Commodities, such as gold, are often negatively correlated with interest rates, as they don't generate income and become relatively less attractive in a rising yield environment.

It is essential for investors to continuously monitor interest rate predictions and central bank policies, as they can significantly impact investment outcomes. However, it's important to recognize that no strategy or prediction is foolproof, and diversification across asset classes and geographic regions remains a prudent approach to mitigate risks and optimize investment returns. Consulting with a financial advisor or considering professional opinions from economists can provide valuable insights for making investment decisions in a rising interest rate environment.

VIII

Future of Investing in a Rising Interest Rate Environment

35

Overview

The future of investing in a rising interest rate environment is a topic of great significance in the field of investing. As interest rates increase, it affects various aspects of the economy, financial markets, and investment strategies. In this overview, we will delve into the implications of rising interest rates on investments and discuss potential strategies to navigate this environment successfully.

Rising interest rates generally occur when central banks intend to curb inflation or cool down an overheated economy. The impact of rising rates varies across different types of investments. Let's explore how this affects some popular investment categories:

1. Bonds:

Rising interest rates can negatively influence bond prices. When rates climb, newly issued bonds offer higher yields, making older bonds with lower rates less attractive. Consequently, existing bonds with fixed interest rates tend to decrease in value. Investors in long-term bonds are particularly vulnerable, as they are locked into lower rates for an extended period. However, shorter-term bonds may fare better due to their lower sensitivity to interest rate changes.

2. Stocks:

Rising interest rates can lead to shifts in investor sentiment and affect stock prices. Companies may face higher borrowing costs, impacting their profitability and growth potential. Industries traditionally sensitive to interest rates, such as financial institutions, homebuilders, and consumer discretionary companies, may experience more pronounced effects. However, it's important to note that rising rates don't always drive down stock prices. Strong economic growth accompanying rate hikes can bolster corporate earnings and support stock valuations.

3. Real Estate:

The real estate market can be significantly impacted by rising interest rates. Higher rates make mortgages more expensive, reducing housing affordability and potentially dampening demand for properties. Consequently, home prices may stagnate or even decline. Real estate investment trusts (REITs) can also be affected as rising rates increase their borrowing costs. However, specific segments of the real estate market may demonstrate resilience, such as commercial properties, which tend to benefit from robust economic conditions.

Navigating the future of investing in a rising interest rate environment requires careful consideration of investment strategies. Here are a few approaches to consider:

1. Diversify:

Maintaining a well-diversified portfolio across different asset classes can help mitigate the impact of rising interest rates on specific investments. By spreading investments across bonds, stocks, real estate, and other assets, you can reduce your exposure to any single category.

2. Focus on shorter-term investments:

As mentioned earlier, shorter-term bonds are less sensitive to interest rate changes. Allocating a portion of your fixed-income investments to instruments with shorter maturities can help minimize potential losses in a rising-rate environment.

3. Employ a tactical approach:

Active management of investment portfolios allows for dynamic adjustments to changing market conditions. In a rising rate environment, you may consider adjusting your asset allocation, emphasizing sectors less affected by interest rates or taking advantage of short-term market opportunities.

4. Seek income from alternative sources:

Rising interest rates can impact traditional income-oriented investments. Exploring alternative income-generating investments, such as dividend-paying stocks, dividend-focused exchange-traded funds (ETFs), or alternative investment strategies, can help diversify income sources and potentially offset declining yields in fixed-income instruments.

5. Stay informed and seek professional advice:

The financial markets and interest rate environment are complex and constantly evolving. Staying updated with current economic trends, following expert opinions, and consulting with a financial advisor can provide valuable insights and guidance tailored to your specific investment goals.

In conclusion, the future of investing in a rising interest rate environment requires careful evaluation and adaptation of investment strategies. Recognizing the potential impact on various asset classes, diversification, tactical adjustments, and seeking alternative income sources can help investors successfully navigate this challenging landscape.

36

Impact of Technological Advancements

The future of investing in a rising interest rate environment is a topic of great significance and interest in the financial world. As interest rates continue to rise, it is crucial for investors to understand the potential impacts and adapt their investment strategies accordingly.

Firstly, it is important to comprehend the relationship between interest rates and investments. In a rising interest rate environment, the cost of borrowing money increases, making it more expensive for companies to finance their operations and fueling higher borrowing costs for individuals. Consequently, this can lead to reduced consumer spending and slower economic growth. As a result, certain sectors, such as real estate and utilities, may experience a decline in profitability and stock prices.

Nevertheless, rising interest rates can also present opportunities for investors. For instance, fixed-income investments, such as bonds, become more attractive as they offer higher yields to compensate for the increased borrowing costs. Additionally, financial institutions like banks may benefit from higher interest rates, as they can earn more on loans and other interest-bearing assets. Therefore, investors need to evaluate the various sectors and asset classes to identify potential winners and losers in a rising interest rate environment.

Furthermore, the impact of technological advancements cannot be overlooked when considering the future of investing. Technological innovations have revolutionized the investing landscape, providing investors with new tools and platforms to make informed decisions. These advancements have led to the rise of robo-advisors, algorithmic trading, and online brokerage platforms, enabling easier and more efficient access to investment opportunities.

Robo-advisors, for instance, use algorithms and artificial intelligence to automatically manage and allocate investment portfolios based on an individual's risk tolerance and financial goals. This automated approach offers cost-effective and personalized investment strategies, making it especially appealing for novice investors or those with limited capital.

Additionally, algorithmic trading, or the use of mathematical models and algorithms to execute trades, has become increasingly prevalent. This form of investing relies on computer-based systems to identify patterns and execute trades at lightning-fast speeds, allowing investors to capitalize on short-term market fluctuations. However, it is important to note that algorithmic trading comes with certain risks, such as system failures or executing trades based on faulty algorithms, which necessitates proper risk management and supervision.

Moreover, technological advancements have also contributed to the growth of online brokerage platforms, offering investors easy access to a wide range of investment options, research tools, and educational resources. These platforms empower individuals to take control of their investments and make informed decisions, encouraging greater financial literacy and participation in the markets.

In conclusion, the future of investing in a rising interest rate environment is influenced by both the impact of rising rates and technological advancements. While rising interest rates may pose challenges to certain sectors, they also present opportunities for investors in areas such as fixed-income investments and financial institutions. Simultaneously, technological advancements have transformed the investing landscape, providing individuals with new tools and platforms to navigate the markets efficiently. Understanding these dynamics and effectively adapting investment strategies to leverage opportunities and mitigate risks will be integral for investors in the coming years.

37

Impact of Global Economic Trends

Investing in a rising interest rate environment can pose unique challenges and opportunities for investors. As global economic trends continue to shift, it is important to understand the potential impact on the future of investing. In this overview, we will explore the key considerations and strategies that investors should keep in mind when faced with rising interest rates in the current global economic landscape.

Firstly, it is crucial to understand the relationship between interest rates and investment performance. In general, rising interest rates tend to have a negative impact on fixed income investments such as bonds and other debt instruments. When interest rates rise, the price of existing bonds tends to fall, as newer bonds with higher interest rates become more attractive to investors. This can result in a decline in the value of bond portfolios.

On the other hand, rising interest rates can benefit certain types of investments. Generally, equities tend to perform well in a rising interest rate environment, as higher rates signal a strengthening economy. Companies with strong fundamentals and solid growth prospects may see their stock prices appreciate in response to higher interest rates. Additionally, sectors such as financials and banking often benefit from rising rates as they can earn more on loans and other interest-earning assets.

However, it is important to note that the impact of rising interest rates on investments is not uniform across all sectors and asset classes. Different industries and regions may have varying degrees of sensitivity to interest rate changes. Thus, it is crucial for investors to conduct thorough analysis and research to identify opportunities and assess potential risks in specific industries or regions.

In the context of global economic trends, it is important to consider the interplay between interest rates, inflation, and central bank policies. Inflation, which is influenced by various factors such as economic growth, supply and demand dynamics, and government policies, can have a significant impact on investment returns. Central banks typically adjust interest rates to control inflation and promote economic stability. Therefore, analyzing global economic trends and understanding central bank policies can help investors anticipate and navigate the impact of rising interest rates.

One important factor to consider is the potential impact of rising interest rates on borrowing costs. As interest rates increase, the cost of borrowing for businesses and consumers also rises. This can lead to reduced spending and potentially slower economic growth. Investors need to assess how rising borrowing costs may influence companies' profitability and consumer behavior, which in turn can affect investment returns.

In terms of investment strategies, diversification remains a key principle regardless of the interest rate environment. By spreading investments across various asset classes, sectors, and regions, investors can reduce their exposure to potential risks associated with rising interest rates. Additionally, investors may consider adjusting the duration (maturity) of fixed income holdings to manage interest rate risk. Shorter-duration bonds typically exhibit lower price sensitivity to interest rate changes compared to longer-duration bonds.

Another strategy to consider is to focus on investments that have historically performed well in rising interest rate environments. This may include sectors such as energy, commodities, and real estate. These sectors often exhibit strong performance when inflation and interest rates rise due to their ability to pass on cost increases or benefit from higher demand.

Lastly, staying informed and regularly reviewing investment portfolios is essential in navigating the future of investing in a rising interest rate environment. Economic conditions and global trends can change rapidly, and investors should continuously assess and adjust their investment strategies as necessary.

In summary, investing in a rising interest rate environment requires careful analysis and consideration of global economic trends. While rising rates can pose challenges to certain types of investments, there are also opportunities to be found. By diversifying portfolios, understanding central bank policies, and focusing on sectors that historically perform well in such environments, investors can position themselves to potentially benefit from rising interest rates while managing associated risks.

About the Author

Clara Capital is a pseudonym for an astute financial analyst with over a decade of experience in the world of finance and investment. With a keen eye for market trends and a passion for educating others, Clara has dedicated herself to helping investors navigate the ever-evolving economic landscape. Her insights are rooted in deep research and real-world experience, making her guidance both practical and invaluable. When she's not analyzing market shifts, Clara enjoys reading historical novels and exploring nature trails.